FRANKIE DETTORI'S

ITALIAN FAMILY COOKBOOK

WIITH MARCO PIERRE WHITE

AND ALEX ANTONIONI

HarperCollins*Publishers*

HarperCollins*Publishers*
77–85 Fulham Palace Road,
Hammersmith, London W6 8JB

The HarperCollins website address
is: www.harpercollins.co.uk

First published by HarperCollins*Publishers* 2007

10 9 8 7 6 5 4 3 2 1

Food photography © Noel Murphy
Location photography © David Munns
Food styling: Calum Watson

A catalogue record of this book is
available from the British Library

ISBN-13 978-0-00-724426-3
ISBN-10 0-00-724426-3

Printed and bound in Italy
by LegoPrint

Additional picture credits: p 28 Vincenzo Lombardo/Taxi/Getty Images;
p 44 Danita Delimont/Alamy; p 48 Angelo Cavalli/Stone/Getty Images;
p 80 Stefano Amantini/4Corners Images; p 84 Nicola Angeli/SIME-4Corners
Images; p 95 De Agostini Picture Library/ Getty Images; p 142 Zoltan
Nagy/SIME-4Corners Images; p 146 Olimpio Fantuz/SIME-4Corners Images;
p 166 Anna Watson/Axiom; p 170 Lonely Planet Images/Getty Images;
p 190 Frances Roberts/Alamy; p 194 Veronique Leplat/4Corners Images;
p 208 Anna Watson/Axiom; p 212 Chuck Pefley/Alamy.

For Catherine, Leo, Ella, Mia, Tallulah and Rocco with all my love.

And for Marco, for helping me to realize my lifelong ambition to be part of the restaurant business. What a partner to have!

Special thanks to Alex Antonioni for all her help picking our brains, and for having the courage to write down closely guarded family recipes. We'd never have got them onto paper without you!

We also couldn't have done without the help of Calum Watson whose patience and resilience is legendary. Thank you, to you, J.C. and the rest of the staff at Frankie's, for making the photo shoots possible.

Thanks also to Efisio Lenti, Head Chef at Ziu Angelini, Porto Pino, Sardinia. Your ravioli is legendary!

Finally, many thanks to Peter Burrell, our long-term agent, business partner and friend. It's been a great ride so far, hasn't it?

INTRODUCTION

Frankie " In Italy, probably more than anywhere else in the world, people live to eat rather than eat to live. All Italians, every single one of them, are passionate about food. In English, if someone is really into food they get called a 'foodie', but in Italian there simply isn't a definitive word for this term. It would never occur to anyone to categorize someone as a foodie – it's a given.

With this kind of attitude you'd think that Italy would be the obesity capital of the world. Yet in spite of being obsessed with food Italians are actually very fussy about what they put in their mouths. Italians simply don't eat processed foods laden with fat, sugar and salt. Instead, 'la vera cucina italiana' is based upon local seasonal produce flavoured with fresh herbs and olive oil. Italians love their food but what they eat isn't unhealthy.

My earliest memories of food and cooking are by most standards fairly sophisticated. My mother's cooking, whilst simple in technique and not given to fussy sauces, was to say the least eclectic. This is because what she cooked on any given day depended on what fresh produce she found at her local market in Milan. This diversity was compounded by the three blissful months we spent in Sardinia with my grandparents every summer. Every day my Nonna would prepare a wonderful array of fresh local produce. This could be anything from line-caught eels and suckling pigs to home-made cheeses and wild boar. All the vegetables she served were fresh out of the ground from her 'orto' (vegetable patch). There were tomatoes the size of a fist that tasted of tomato in a way that I've never tasted since, figs so ripe they dripped with syrup, huge succulent peaches and the sweetest grapes I've ever tasted. Best of all, my grandparents produced thirty litres of olive oil every year from their own trees. I can still remember the excitement of helping to pick the olives as a young boy. That, my friend, is living.

My point is that Italians don't go in for the 'chicken nugget' version of kid's food – I ate what the adults ate and learned to love and respect the provenance of food from a very young age. It's not unusual in Italy for five- or six-year-old kids to start drinking a little wine mixed with water, especially if it is 'fatt'in casa' (homemade), i.e. with Nonno treading the grapes. I think this contributes hugely to fact that Italian kids don't binge drink. They are so used to being around alcohol that it negates the mystery and disposes with the 'it's naughty so I'll do it' issue.

I'm happy to say that my kids love their food and are not fussy, finicky eaters. I'm sure this is because they eat proper food, not so called children's food. Sure, Catherine tries to sneak in extra vegetables here and there but overall they do OK. My son Leo will try anything once. We gave him prawns the other day and he loved them. There was even a time when all he wanted for breakfast was fish – he's clearly his father's son! It's also important for me that my kids recognise their Italian roots, so we eat a lot of Italian in my house, balancing it out with the odd shepherd's pie and bangers and mash, which I also love.

This book is all about bringing good food into your home. My mission, and yours if you choose to accept it (I've always wanted to say that!), is to get families to sit down together to enjoy great food and, more importantly, each other's company on a regular basis. Sunday lunch in my house is sacrosanct – woe betide anyone who doesn't show. It's the one day of the week we all catch up on each other's news, gossip and the good and not so good bits of the week that was.

My kitchen at home is completely open plan and is in fact an extension of the dining room and playroom, which in turn lead into the garden. When I cook at home there are always least half a dozen people milling around me (as well as assorted cats and dogs) playing, talking, tasting, laughing, bickering and, of course, opening the odd bottle of wine. When the food is ready everyone sits down together and I get a nice warm feeling in my bones, being surrounded by those I love.

As they say in Italy, 'La cosa più importante e mangiar in famiglia, così si capisce tutto di tutto', which roughly translated means, 'the most important thing in life is to eat together as family: only then can you comprehend what's really going on the lives of the people closest to you'. I have a funny feeling that these wise words will prove invaluable when my kids are teenagers. ,,

Frankie Dettori

Marco " The greatest culinary influence in my life came from having an Italian mother who was a natural-born cook. Her family lived just outside Genoa where I used to spend my summer holidays as a little boy. My earliest food memories are of my mother picking me up from the school gates at midday to go home for lunch. I must have been about five years old. It was only ever the two of us and I'm not sure why my elder brother didn't join us and instead stayed on for school dinners. Maybe she still regarded me as 'the baby' – or perhaps she had already spotted my interest in food. When we ate we'd talk and giggle our way through lunch. I think the reason this had such a lasting impression on me is that those simple meals were always filled with happiness.

Mum cooked simple food intelligently and with great deal of attention to detail. She always used seasonal produce. In winter she'd make hearty soups with root vegetables, pulses and a little rice or pasta with a sprinkling of Parmigiano. In summer we'd have delicate broths studded with podded peas and lots fresh, soft herbs or perhaps a vegetable rice salad or simple spaghetti 'al burro' (which remains to this day my favourite pasta). She steered clear of fussy food and heavy sauces. Sometimes lunch would be just a very ripe tomato with a little salt, olive oil and, perhaps, some bread or a piece of cheese. But even a simple snack like this was made with love and a great deal of care and thus still lingers in my memory. Her food philosophy was to buy the best quality that you can afford and to let the flavours speak for themselves.

I believe my mother's inherent understanding and appreciation of food is a major component in the DNA of most, if not all Italian women. They seem to posses an uncanny knowledge and love for cooking and its ability to nurture. Italians always adhere to the principle that a great meal is not about expensive ingredients. On the contrary, some of the best food in Italy stems from 'la cucina povera', 'the kitchen of the poor', which understands the importance of allowing Mother Nature to do her job as supplier of our groceries, meat and fish. All that is left for the cook to do is to present her produce in the purest and simplest way.

My mother died when I was six, leaving my father, a chef, to look after three young boys traumatised by their loss and in need of stability and love. My old man wasn't an outwardly affectionate father but he was always very correct and dependable. He demonstrated his love for us in the way he knew best, through food.

We had very little spare money and fortunately, with hindsight, we were too poor to buy the tinned produce that was so fashionable at the time. Dad had always cooked a little at home, but his forte had been full English breakfasts at weekends. Now that he was stuck with all the cooking he expected all of us to muck in. We were dispatched to pick apples, forage for rhubarb and collect blackberries. As soon as we were old enough to learn how, he also sent us out to shoot rabbits and hares, and to fish for eels, trout or anything else we could land. Nothing went to waste, everything got eaten. We hunted to feed the family, not for leisure and it ignited a passion for hunting and fishing that remains with me to this day. It is my belief that before you can be a great cook you have to understand the providence of food and respect Mother Nature and her bounty.

Today, the most important thing in my life is my kids. Nothing comes before my family. Nothing. In my three Michelin star days I cooked with my ego and not with my heart in order to gain and keep those oh-so-precious stars. I was rarely at home with my kids. They would come to see me between services at my restaurant in the Hyde Park Hotel for about half an hour every day, which wasn't very satisfactory for any of us. In fact, my children are the reason I took the momentous decision to give back my stars. It was the only way I could spend a lot more time with them. My little ones mean the whole world to me – certainly more than three Michelin stars ever could.

I would like this book to get families back round the dinner table and eating good food. Don't just buy the book, have a quick flick through, then stick it back on the shelf with all your other glossy celebrity-endorsed cookbooks. This is not what Frankie and I are trying to achieve. Use it, note the recipes that Frankie and I loved as kids, which in turn are loved in equal measure by our own children, and try them out on *your* kids. Educating your children on the joy of good food and eating well is as important a duty for parents as teaching them good manners and how to love each other.

If this book ends up covered in flour and sticky finger prints and with the odd note in the margin, then and only then will you have realized its true value. 〞

Marco Pierre White

FRANKIE'S BAR AND GRILL

Frankie **"** Sometimes in life we find ourselves in the right place at the right time doing stuff we didn't imagine we would ever get involved in. The first time I ever met Marco was when I popped into Drones, one of his restaurants in London, for a quick bite before heading home. He was also there having dinner and came over to join us for a glass of wine. The conversation soon turned to food and restaurants.

London is positively teeming with restaurants, there is no doubt about that. Every possible permutation and nationality of cuisine known to mankind is widely available, yet I'd always found it hard to find good family-friendly restaurants which are 'happy meal' or kiddie menu-free zones. I suddenly found myself in a heated conversation with Marco. Why aren't there more restaurants that cater for families? Why don't the ones that exist serve real food that all the family will love? I don't serve my kids frozen chicken nuggets at home, so why would I go to a restaurant to pay for the privilege of doing so? And why can't family restaurants be stylish enough to keep the grown-ups happy but also informal enough so we can relax there with all the kids? What I wanted was a bit of family glamour! Who would have thought that my passionate outcry would be instrumental in bringing a touch of Italian family values and lifestyle to a series of restaurants?

As a jockey I have to be extremely disciplined about what I eat. They say that men think about sex once every seven minutes. Well, not this man! It's food I can't stop thinking about. And as

I can't eat what I want when I'm racing, my next favourite thing is to talk food. Doing just that with a charismatic, incredibly knowledgeable, three-starred Michelin chef was, for me, pure paradise. Marco and I spent the next couple of hours coming up with a wish list of what our perfect family restaurant would offer, from the décor and the general feel of the place to which of our favourite family recipes we'd make sure were on the menu. It was a fantastic evening.

I left Marco at Drones around 11pm, having enjoyed some of the best carpaccio I had ever eaten along with a glass of my favourite Italian red wine, Sassicaia. (It was just the one glass, but it meant I had to run an extra fifteen minutes in a ski suit the next morning to burn it off. I kid you not!)

Marco called me the next day. He had, literally overnight, come up with a blueprint for a family restaurant called Frankie's (how flattering is that?) and asked me to go into business with him. The concept that he had come up with was pure genius and I didn't hesitate to say 'I do'. Thus the unlikely marriage of Frankie Dettori, little Italian jockey and (whenever possible) bon viveur, and Marco Pierre White, Michelin-starred chef and infamous raconteur, came to be.

The incredible thing about Marco is that once he has the bones of a great idea he is capable of turning it into a reality in double-quick time. And so it was that Frankie's was born three months later in Knightsbridge, London, with everything I had been looking for in a family restaurant – and so much more I didn't even know I'd wanted until I got it.

The décor was entirely down to Marco, as it is with all of his restaurants, for, despite employing an army of designers and experts, ultimately most of the ideas come from him. He has a remarkable eye for detail and seems to know instinctively what works and what doesn't. For Frankie's he wanted a classical look that would exude fun with that all-important shot of glamour. He lined every inch of wall space with floor-to-ceiling mirrors then hung six huge glitter balls from the ceiling. The finished product was awesome, a perfect blend of tradition and fun that just oozes glamour.

Everyone fell in love with the four-foot wide glitter balls, me and the kids included. In fact, we liked them so much I nicked one and it's now hanging in the TV room at home, all four feet of it. My wife Catherine was less than convinced it belongs there, but she was outvoted four to one. Democracy is a wonderful thing, especially when the kids are on your side!

Frankie's opening night was a star-studded event. Madonna and Guy Ritchie (now regular customers), Claudia Schiffer and Matthew Vaughn, Philip Green and Larry David were there, to name but a few, and from that very first night Frankie's created a buzz that has increased in volume to a now deafening roar. In the space of two short years we have opened three more Frankie's restaurants in London: in Selfridges, Chiswick and Putney. We have just opened up in Dubai and Shanghai as well, with plans for Las Vegas in the pipeline. Amazing.

I was in Frankie's with my brood just a few days ago and when I looked around the restaurant it warmed the cockles of my little Italian heart to see tables of families of all age groups, from grandparents to toddlers, laughing, eating, drinking and having a great time. 'We've done it,' I thought, 'now there really is a great restaurant for families.' 🙶

Marco 66 The night Frankie popped into Drones for a quick supper was the catalyst for an idea which had been brewing in me for some time: to open a family restaurant that would serve good food with a lot of fun and a little bit of glamour thrown in for good measure. When Frankie and I got talking, I knew I'd found the perfect partner for my venture. His vision of what a good family restaurant should offer and his absolute faith that 'la famiglia' is the central component of life mirrored my own. We also had the perfect research group available to us. Between us we had two wives, three grandmothers, two grandfathers and, most important of all, eight kids aged between one and seventeen who all had very clear ideas of their own about what they wanted from a restaurant.

When it came to the menu Frankie and I followed my mother's philosophy of buying the best and allowing the ingredients to speak for themselves. As well as classical Italian dishes, such as pizza, pasta and the traditional meat and fish, I was also keen to have a good quality burger on the menu along with a few unusual additions, like roast belly of pork and the much underrated calf's tongue.

Of course, the restaurant business is not just about food: it's also about entertainment. I wanted to make sure that everyone who ate at Frankie's would be a little happier when they left than when they came in. With the help of Jean Cristoph, my operations director, and Calum Watson, my executive chef, we turned Frankie's from an idea into a reality. Two years on, given the amount of families we have coming through the doors every week, it would seem we have achieved our goal. 99

CHEF'S NOTE

When cooking I don't always season with salt, especially
when it comes to meat; I like to season using chicken stock cubes
(Knorr is my preference). I add a pinch or two when cooking
vegetable soups and all meat sauces and gravies. Firstly, this is
more forgiving than salt and, secondly, when finishing sauces
you don't have reduce them as much to reach their desired
flavour. This makes the finished product lighter rather than
over-reduced and over-strong in natural salt.

When cooking vegetables, a crumbled cube in the water
vastly improves their flavour. Another great use is when
roasting a chicken: create a light paste using chicken stock
cubes and some olive oil, then spread this over the breast of
the chicken and inside the cavity walls of the bird, rather
than seasoning with lots of salt.

Too many chefs turn their noses up at certain products,
but when you think about it a burger is not a burger without
ketchup; an English breakfast is not a breakfast without HP
sauce; fish and chips are not the same without malt vinegar;
and that great British institution the ham sandwich is not a
proper ham sandwich without English mustard.

Let's not forget that good food is all about flavour, so never be
afraid to cook with these products. Many acclaimed restaurants
have these ingredients and more in their dry goods stores and
chefs use them freely and without compunction.

Good eating.

Marco Pierre White

E' SARDA, E' MURRU.

SALUMIFICIO
MURRU
Irgoli

1965 · 2005

40 ANNI DI PASSIONE PER LA BONTÀ

ANTIPASTI
STARTERS

PROSCIUTTO DI PARMA CON FICHI

Parma ham with figs

LINGUA DI VITELLO CON
MOSTARDA DI CREMONA

Cold calf's tongue with Mostarda di Cremona

CARPACCIO CON MOSTARDA

Carpaccio of beef with a mustard dressing

COZZE ALLA MARINARA

Moules à la marinière

MINESTRA DI LENTICCHIE

Lentil soup

MOZZARELLA DI BUFALA CAPRESE

Mozzarella and tomato salad

MINESTRONE DI VERDURA

Minestrone soup

STRACCIATELLA

Stracciatella 'egg-drop' soup

PASTA E FAGIOLI

Pasta and bean soup

PEPERONI FARCITI AL TONNO

Roast bell peppers with tuna, pine nuts and olives

COZZE RIPIENE

Baked stuffed mussels

PROSCIUTTO DI PARMA CON FICHI

Parma ham with figs

24 finely cut slices of Parma ham
4 ripe figs, peeled and quartered

Serves: 4
Preparation time: 5 minutes

Divide the Parma ham between 4
plates. Place the figs in the centre,
and serve.

Marco *" This dish reminds me of happy days
spent with my mother's sister, Zia Luciana,
in Genoa. I love the wonderful combination of slightly salty
ham with sweet figs. Buy your prosciutto from a good Italian
delicatessen and have it sliced paper-thin off the bone in front
of you. The figs, either green or black, should be soft to the
touch. I believe in sourcing the very best ingredients and
allowing the food to speak for itself, without the need for
anything else on the plate, even seasoning. "*

LINGUA DI VITELLO CON MOSTARDA DI CREMONA

Cold calf's tongue with Mostarda di Cremona

1 calf's tongue
1 carrot, peeled and roughly
    chopped
1 onion, halved
2 celery sticks, roughly choped
1 whole bulb of garlic, halved
1 bay leaf
1 small jar of Mostarda di
    Cremona, fruits chopped and
    syrup reserved

FOR THE SALSA DI ERBE:
a handful of fresh basil leaves
a handful of fresh flat leaf parsley
1 anchovy fillet
3 tablespoons Parmesan
3 tablespoons extra virgin olive oil
1 dessert spoon lemon juice
sea salt and freshly ground black
    pepper

Serves: 8
Soaking time: 48 hours
Preparation time: 10 mins
Cooking time: 3½ hours

To prepare the tongue for cooking, soak it in cold water for 48 hours, changing the water at least every 6 to 8 hours.

Combine all the Salsa di Erbe ingredients in a food processor, and whiz until it is the consistency of thin cream.

After soaking, place the calf's tongue in a large pan of cold water, bring to the boil, then refresh under cold running water. Place the tongue back in the saucepan, and add the carrot, onion, celery, garlic and bay leaf. Cover with cold water, bring to the boil, then reduce the heat and simmer for 3½ hours. Remove the tongue, peel off the outer skin (it should come away quite easily) and then refresh under cold water. Once cooled, slice it thinly.

To serve, spoon the Salsa di Erbe on to 4 plates and then add a layer of the thinly sliced tongue. Sprinkle over the chopped Mostarda di Cremona and a little of its accompanying syrup.

Frankie " I ate this dish many times when growing up in Milan, so I was keen to have it on the menu at Frankie's. Calf's tongue is Italian peasant cooking at its finest and Mostarda di Cremona, which is available in most Italian delis, contains whole fruits that have been steeped in a clear, sugary syrup, laced with pure mustard. The end product packs quite a punch, akin to the Japanese horseradish Wasabi, although the Mostarda of my youth seemed less sweet and a helluva lot stronger. "

CARPACCIO CON MOSTARDA

Carpaccio of beef with a mustard dressing

200 g fillet of organic Aberdeen
   Angus beef
extra virgin olive oil
4 handfuls of wild rocket, washed
   and dried thoroughly

FOR THE DRESSING:

1 egg yolk
2 teaspoons Dijon mustard
2 teaspoons coarse-grain mustard
1 teaspoon lemon juice
a dash of Worcestershire sauce
200 ml vegetable oil
sea salt

Serves: 4
Preparation time: 15 minutes
Chilling time: 2 hours

Wrap the beef fillet tightly in cling film and place in a freezer for approximately 2 hours.

For the dressing, whisk the egg yolk with the Dijon and coarse-grain mustard, lemon juice and Worcestershire sauce. Then slowly pour in the vegetable oil, whisking all the time. Season with the salt.

To serve, remove the beef fillet from the freezer, unwrap it and – using a very sharp, serrated knife – slice it as finely as you can. (Your fillet should yield approximately 32 slices.) Divide the beef slices between 4 plates and brush lightly with the olive oil, using a pastry brush. Drizzle with the mustard dressing and scatter over the rocket leaves.

Frankie " This is the dish that brought me and Marco together for the first time. To me, it's the perfect supper for when I come home late from a day's racing, as it's relatively light but the meat and the intense flavours of the dressing are satisfying. I eat this as a main course, although in most Italian households it's regarded as a starter, served with a few mixed leaves and a nice glass of red. "

COZZE ALLA MARINARA

Moules à la marinière

200 g unsalted butter
200 ml extra virgin olive oil
8 sprigs of fresh thyme
1 garlic clove, crushed
½ medium onion, finely chopped
1 fresh red chilli, de-seeded and
    finely chopped
1 kg fresh mussels, washed and
    de-bearded
3 tablespoons white wine

Serves: 4
Preparation time: 10 minutes
Cooking time: 10 minutes

Whisk the butter in a food processor, until doubled in volume and light and creamy. Trickle in the olive oil, keeping the food processor going, until the oil is fully incorporated. Pick off the leaves from 4 of the thyme sprigs and mix into the olive oil mixture with the garlic.

In a large saucepan, add the onion, chilli, mussels and white wine. Cover with a lid and cook over a medium heat until all the mussels have opened (the big mussels will take longer than the small ones). Pour off half the cooking liquid, then stir in the butter and olive oil mixture. To serve, divide the mussels between 4 bowls, spoon over the juices and garnish with the reserved sprigs of thyme.

Marco " Mussels make a wonderful meal. My dad loved cooking mussels so I think of it as quite a male dish. It seems to be popular now to serve mussels with very finely cut chips. But, for my money, the only way to eat mussels is untidily, discarding shells as you go, with a good hunk of fresh bread to mop up all those gorgeous winey, fishy juices at the bottom of the bowl. "

MINESTRA DI LENTICCHIE

Lentil soup

1 kg puy lentils
3 tablespoons extra virgin olive oil
3 carrots, roughly chopped
2 celery sticks, roughly chopped
2 leeks, roughly chopped
3 shallots, roughly chopped
10 fresh sage leaves
1½ litres water
sea salt and freshly ground pepper
4 tablespoons finely grated
  Parmesan, to serve
4 tablespoons extra virgin olive oil,
  to serve

FOR THE VEGETABLE STOCK
  (MAKES 1½ LITRES):
2 carrots
1 large onion
2 celery sticks
1 bay leaf
1 whole garlic bulb, halved
6 peppercorns
2 leeks, whites only
3 litres water

Serves: 4
Preparation time: 20 minutes
Cooking time: 1¼ hours

Put all the ingredients for the vegetable stock into a large saucepan, bring to the boil, then reduce the heat and simmer for 30 minutes. Strain through a sieve and set aside.

Soak the lentils in cold water overnight, then refresh under a running tap. In a large saucepan, heat the olive oil, add the carrots, celery, leeks and shallots and gently cook over a low heat until softened. Add the lentils, sage leaves, vegetable stock and water, bring to the boil and then simmer for 45 minutes until the lentils are soft to the bite. Transfer to a blender and liquidize until smooth. Season to taste. Serve in warmed bowls and top each with a tablespoon of Parmesan and olive oil.

Marco " Italians love their hearty vegetable soups. We don't go in for simple consommés, as we like our soups with big flavours and lots of texture. This is one of my favourites and, again, it all comes down to the quality of the ingredients. I remember sitting in my mother's kitchen watching her chop the vegetables and, as the dish took shape and started to bubble on the stove, somehow, all felt right with the world. "

13

MOZZARELLA DI BUFALA CAPRESE

Mozzarella and tomato salad

4 x 125 g balls of Mozzarella di
  Bufala
2 ripe avocados
12 cherry tomatoes, halved
16 basil leaves
4 tablespoons extra virgin olive oil
sea salt

Serves: 4
Preparation time: 10 minutes

Place a mozzarella ball in the centre of each plate. Peel and quarter the avocados and place 2 quarters either side of the mozzarella balls. Then add the cherry tomatoes and basil leaves. To serve, drizzle over the olive oil and season with sea salt.

Frankie " This dish must be on every Italian restaurant menu in the world, and when done correctly, it's the best. The most important thing to remember is that the ingredients must be absolutely tip top. Mozzarella di Bufala is easy to find in most delis and is a world away from the Danish mozzarella available in most supermarkets. The tomatoes also need to be ripe and fragrant, the basil fresh and aromatic, and the avocados well ripened. If not, turn the page and make another dish! "

MINESTRONE DI VERDURA

Minestrone soup

225 g dried cannellini beans

3 tablespoons extra virgin olive oil

1 medium onion, chopped

1 medium carrot, chopped

½ celery stick, plus a handful of the celery leaves, chopped

225 g ripe tomatoes, skinned and roughly chopped

½ teaspoon sugar

1¼ litres water

500 g broad beans, shelled

225 g spring greens or green cabbage, shredded

50 g short pasta (such as penne, macaroni, fusilli)

1 generous handful of chopped fresh flat leaf parsley

sea salt and freshly ground black pepper

lots of freshly grated Parmesan, to serve

4 tablespoons extra virgin olive oil, to serve

Serves: 4
Preparation time: 20 minutes
Soaking time: overnight
Cooking time: 55 minutes

Soak the cannellini beans in cold water overnight. Then drain, place in a heavy-bottomed pan, cover with cold water, bring to the boil, drain and refresh under a cold running tap. Set aside.

Heat the olive oil in a large saucepan. Add the onion, carrot and celery and cook gently over a low heat for about 15 minutes, until softened. Add the tomatoes and the sugar, and simmer for a further 10 minutes, stirring often. Pour in the water and bring to the boil. Reduce the heat, cover and simmer for 20 minutes, skimming off any foam that may rise to the surface.

Add the cannellini beans, broad beans, spring greens (or cabbage), pasta and parsley, and simmer for a further 8 minutes, or until the pasta is cooked. Season with salt and pepper. To serve, ladle into warmed bowls, stir in a tablespoon of olive oil and sprinkle with the freshly grated Parmesan.

Frankie " The classic Italian soup, that is so much more than just a bowl of soup. To me, it evokes a feeling of well-being and a time when families ate together, when Sunday lunches were sacrosanct and when my nonna's minestrone soup was on the menu. She would pick all the vegetables and herbs from her own vegetable plot and would take hours cleaning and chopping the ingredients. The end result, with a sprinkling of Parmigiano cheese, was just heaven. "

17

STRACCIATELLA

Stracciatella 'egg-drop' soup

3 medium eggs
2 teaspoons finely chopped fresh
    flat leaf parsley
3 tablespoons grated Parmesan
1 teaspoon lemon juice
1 litre chicken stock
sea salt

Serves: 4
Preparation time: 5 minutes
Cooking time: 5 minutes

Whisk the eggs with the parsley, Parmesan and lemon juice. Place the chicken stock in a saucepan and bring to a rolling boil.

Using a metal spoon, slowly pour in the egg mixture, stirring all the time, so that long ribbons of egg are formed.

Season to taste, take off the heat and serve in warmed bowls immediately.

Frankie " This is a get-well-soon, cuddle-in-a-bowl, cure-all soup. Based on the classic Italian brodo (chicken stock), this is our version of the famous Jewish penicillin. The addition of lightly beaten eggs and Parmigiano cheese is inspired. "

PASTA E FAGIOLI

Pasta and bean soup

300 g dried cannellini beans
3 garlic cloves
a sprig of fresh sage
8 tablespoons extra virgin olive oil
300 g dried short pasta (such as
    macaroni, fusilli)
a sprig of fresh rosemary
½ small fresh red chilli pepper,
    roughly chopped
sea salt and freshly ground black
    pepper
a large handful of freshly grated
    Parmesan

Serves: 4
Preparation time: 10 minutes
Cooking time: 2 hours 15 minutes
Soaking time: overnight

Soak the beans in cold water overnight. Then drain, refresh and place in a saucepan with 2 of the garlic cloves, the sage and 2 tablespoons of the olive oil. Cover with cold water, bring to a gentle simmer, then cover with a lid and cook over a low heat for 2 hours, or until the beans are soft and well cooked. (Check the water level during cooking and add more as required.) Drain and discard the sage sprig and garlic cloves, and keep warm.

Meanwhile, cook the pasta in a large pan of salted boiling water, according to the packet instructions. While the pasta is cooking, heat 5 tablespoons of the olive oil in a saucepan and gently fry the rosemary sprig, remaining garlic clove and chilli for 5 minutes. Then remove and discard the rosemary, garlic and chilli and pour the remaining olive oil over the beans. When the pasta is ready, drain it in a colander, reserving a little of the cooking water. Combine the pasta with the beans, add a little of the reserved cooking water, season, and then sprinkle on the Parmesan.

Frankie " I love pasta e fagioli. It's a really warming dish and perfect for when I've just come back from a hard day's training. It's incredibly soporific; a bowl of this and a glass of red wine, and I'm out for the count! Not one for when I'm racing but just the thing for when it's wet and cold and blowing a gale outside. "

PEPERONI FARCITI AL TONNO

Roast bell peppers with tuna, pine nuts and olives

4 large red Romano peppers
4 tablespoons pine nuts
100 g canned Italian or Spanish
    tuna, in olive oil, drained
20 green olives, stoned and
    chopped
a large pinch of dried chilli flakes
3 tablespoons lemon juice
extra virgin olive oil
sea salt and freshly ground black
    pepper

Serves: 4–6
Preparation time: 30 minutes
Cooking time: 20 minutes

Preheat the oven to 180°C/350°F/Gas Mark 4. Place the peppers in the oven and roast for 20 minutes. Then remove the skin, de-seed them and cut into quarters lengthways.

While the peppers are roasting, toast the pine nuts on a baking tray in the oven until they begin to change colour (about 2 minutes).

In a bowl, mix the tuna, olives, pine nuts and chilli flakes with the lemon juice. Place a tablespoon of the tuna mixture on the inner side of each pepper quarter, and roll inwards to form a tube. Place on a serving dish, with the join of the pepper facing down.

Drizzle with some olive oil, season with salt and pepper, and serve.

Frankie " The one time of year I'm pretty relaxed about what I eat is when I'm on holiday in Sardinia with my family and friends. This makes a lovely light lunch or supper, and is a great dish if I've been overdoing the carbs or indulging in Mr Ravioli's homemade pasta! "

COZZE RIPIENE

Baked stuffed mussels

2 kg fresh mussels
100 g spinach leaves
3 tablespoons grated Parmesan
4 garlic cloves, chopped
grated zest of 1 lemon
1 egg, beaten
sea salt and freshly ground pepper
50 g natural breadcrumbs
4 tablespoons extra virgin olive oil

Preheat the oven to 200°C/400°F/Gas Mark 6.

Wash the mussels well, de-beard them and put them in a large saucepan. Cook over a medium heat until they all open (no need to add water as the wetness from the washing will be sufficient). Discard any that don't open, remove the meat and reserve the shells.

Steam or cook the spinach leaves in boiling water for a minute or two, roughly chop them and place in a bowl. Add the Parmesan, garlic, lemon zest, egg and seasoning, and mix well. Place each mussel on a half shell and cover with a generous dollop of the Parmesan and spinach mixture. Sprinkle on the breadcrumbs and drizzle over the olive oil. Bake for 10 minutes. Serve while still hot.

Serves: 4
Preparation time: 10 minutes
Cooking time: 10 minutes

Frankie " There's something irresistible about eating mussels in Italy; they just taste different. It could be because I remember as a boy collecting mussels from the beach and then rushing home to give them to my mother for that evening's meal. This is how my mum cooks mussels. If, like me, you need to avoid carbohydrates, leave out the breadcrumbs, although they do add a really nice crunch. "

INSALATE

SALADS

INSALATA DI RUCOLA E PARMIGIANO
Rocket and Gran Padano salad

INSALATA DI PERA, CICORIA E GORGONZOLA
Chicory, pear, walnut and Gorgonzola salad

TONNO E FAGIOLI
Tuna and bean salad

VITELLO TONNATO
Cold veal with a tuna and caper sauce

INSALATA ALLA TORPINO
Walnut, spinach and pomegranate salad

INDIVIA CON ACCIUGHE
Warm endive salad with garlic and anchovies

INSALATA DI PATATINE, ROSMARINO, POMODORINI E OLIVE
Warm salad of sautéed rosemary potatoes
with cherry tomatoes and black olives

INSALATA AL BALSAMICO
Sautéed Prosciutto di Parma
and balsamic vinegar salad

INSALATA DI PISELLI
Fresh green pea salad

INSALATA DI RUCOLA E PARMIGIANO

Rocket and Gran Padano salad

8 handfuls of wild rocket
65 g Parmigiano di Gran Padano,
 thinly shaved

FOR THE DRESSING:
150 ml extra virgin olive oil
3 tablespoons balsamic vinegar
a small pinch of sugar and salt

Serves: 4
Preparation time: 5 minutes

For the dressing, whisk the olive oil into the balsamic vinegar very slowly, until emulsified. Season with a small pinch of sugar and salt. To serve, place the rocket leaves in a bowl and drizzle over the dressing. Top with the shaved Parmesan.

Marco " This brilliant Italian salad became wildly popular in London restaurants a few years ago. And this was when chefs started mucking about with it, adding all manner of things, such as pine nuts, bacon, croutons or, God help me, poached eggs. I don't add anything as this dish stands up on its own either as a starter or light lunch, or as an accompaniment to a grilled or roasted meat dish. "

INSALATA DI PERA, CICORIA E GORGONZOLA

Chicory, pear, walnut and Gorgonzola salad

100 g caster sugar

2 ripe Conference pears, peeled and chopped into 1 cm cubes

4 heads of yellow chicory, halved and with the bitter core cut out, and thinly sliced lengthways

40 g walnuts, roughly chopped

100 g Gorgonzola, cut into 1 cm cubes

FOR THE DRESSING:

25 g walnuts

3 tablespoons white wine vinegar

150 ml walnut oil

a pinch of sugar

salt

Serves: 4
Preparation time: 10 minutes
Cooking time: 10 minutes

To make the dressing, place the walnuts and white wine vinegar in a food processor and, with the motor running, trickle in the walnut oil until emulsified. Add a pinch of sugar and season to taste.

Sprinkle the caster sugar into a pan and cook over a high heat for a few seconds until the sugar begins to caramelize and turn golden brown. Then add the cubed pears and cook for 10 minutes until they begin to caramelize. Remove from the heat and leave to cool. To serve, place the sliced chicory, walnuts and Gorgonzola in a bowl, add the caramelized pears and sugar, mix in the dressing and divide between 4 plates or bowls.

Marco " When I bring the kids to Frankie's for an early supper, I always try to eat with them and this is one of my favourite light suppers. Gorgonzola is a fantastic cheese – it has the bite of a good Stilton, tempered with the creaminess of a Taleggio, and is perfect with the crunchy walnuts and sweet pears. "

TONNO E FAGIOLI

Tuna and bean salad

400 g good quality tinned Italian or
   Spanish tuna in olive oil, drained
3 tablespoons lemon juice
100 ml extra virgin olive oil
1 red onion, sliced very finely
a handful of fresh basil leaves
sea salt and freshly ground black
   pepper

FOR THE FLAGEOLET BEANS:
400 g flageolet beans, soaked
   overnight
1 carrot, halved
½ onion
1 celery stick
½ bulb of garlic
2 sprigs of fresh thyme
1 bay leaf

Serves: 4
Preparation time: 10 minutes
Cooking time: 2 hours

Place the soaked flageolet beans in a saucepan, cover with cold water, bring to the boil, then drain and refresh under a cold running tap. Place the beans back into the saucepan, then add the carrot, onion, celery, garlic, thyme and bay leaf. Cover with cold water, bring to the boil, then lower the heat and simmer for 2 hours, until the beans are softened. Remove the vegetables, drain the beans and refresh under cold running water.

Place the beans in a bowl and combine with the tuna, lemon juice and olive oil. Divide between 4 serving bowls, top with the finely sliced onion and basil leaves, and season to taste.

Frankie " My aunt used to make this dish for an antipasto or for Saturday lunch, served with green salad and warm bread. Tinned, not fresh, tuna works best here but don't use the cheaper tins packed in brine. Italian tuna in olive oil is worth the extra money, has a completely different texture and is packed with flavour. "

VITELLO TONNATO

Cold veal with a tuna and caper sauce

500 g topside of veal
1 celery stick
1 carrot
1 medium bunch of fresh flat leaf
   parsley
sea salt

FOR THE SAUCE:

2 eggs
a pinch of salt
60 ml extra virgin olive oil
150 g tinned tuna in olive oil,
   drained
2 anchovy fillets in olive oil,
   drained
1 tablespoon capers (plus a little
   extra to serve), drained and salt
   rinsed off
juice of 1 lemon
60 ml milk

Serves: 4
Preparation time: 20 minutes
Cooking time: 2 hours

In a large saucepan, bring 1.7 litres of water to the boil. Add the veal, celery, carrot, parsley and a pinch of salt and simmer for 2 hours over a low heat. Drain the veal and set aside to cool. Once cooled, slice the veal very thinly and arrange in overlapping layers on an oval platter.

To make the sauce, separate the yolk from 1 of the eggs. Place the egg yolk in a food processor and combine with the remaining whole egg and a pinch of salt. Then, with the motor running, slowly add the olive oil in a thin stream. When a mayonnaise consistency forms, add the tuna, anchovies, capers, lemon juice and milk. Blend to a creamy consistency. To serve, pour the sauce over the cooled, sliced meat and sprinkle over a few more capers.

Frankie " I always associate this elegant dish with my first girlfriend, Giovanna. Her family invited, or should I say summoned, me to lunch and when I arrived her elder twin brothers, both well-built and far more worldly-wise than me, let me know, in the nicest possible way, what they would do to me if I in any way hurt or, God forbid, disrespected their little sister. Fortunately their mother was an excellent cook and we were soon relaxing over lunch as if the conversation had never taken place. The memory of her Vitello Tonnato lasted a lot longer than my relationship with Giovanna! "

37

INSALATA ALLA TORPINO

Walnut, spinach and pomegranate salad

1 head of chicory
1 head of red radicchio
100 g baby spinach leaves
1 fennel bulb
1 bunch of radishes
100 g Parmigiano, finely shaved
   into curls
1 pomegranate
sea salt
1 tablespoon red wine vinegar
4 tablespoons extra virgin olive oil
125 g walnuts, chopped

Serves: 4
Preparation time: 5 minutes

Separate the leaves of the chicory and radicchio, discarding their cores and any damaged outer leaves. Wash the chicory, radicchio and baby spinach leaves and pat dry. Then roughly tear the leaves by hand and place in a bowl. Clean, top and tail and finely slice the fennel and radishes, and add to the salad leaves with the Parmigiano. Then, halve the pomegranate, scoop out the seeds and add to the salad bowl.

Dissolve a good grinding of sea salt in the red wine vinegar, add the olive oil, mix well, and pour over the salad. Toss thoroughly, sprinkle with the walnuts and serve.

Frankie " This is a wonderful combination of all my favourite salad ingredients. The walnuts and Parmigiano cheese give it lots of texture and crunch, and radicchio is an Italian staple – a member of the chicory family with a slightly bitter, nutty taste. This recipe came from an old Italian cookbook and is apparently from Campania, the supposed capital of southern Italian cuisine. "

INDIVIA CON ACCIUGHE

Warm endive salad with garlic and anchovies

4 heads of endive
2 tablespoons olive oil
2 garlic cloves, crushed
5 anchovy fillets, drained of their
    oil and chopped
a handful of fresh mint and parsley
    leaves, roughly chopped
salt and freshly ground black
    pepper

Serves: 4
Preparation time: 15 minutes
Cooking time: 5 minutes

Cook the heads of endive in lightly boiling salted water for around 5–8 minutes depending on their size; they should be just tender. Test with a very sharp knife, and do not allow the endive to become too soft. Drain and refresh under cold water. Allow to cool.

Cut the endive heads in half lengthways and lay them face down on kitchen roll to soak up any excess water.

Heat the olive oil in a large frying pan and add the crushed garlic cloves. Cook over a medium heat until the garlic is golden brown, then remove the garlic and add the anchovies and cook, stirring, until they disintegrate into the oil.

Place the endive halves face down in the pan and cook for about 5 minutes, until golden. Gently turn the endive halves over, add the mint and parsley to the pan, season to taste and serve piping hot from the pan, with lots of crusty bread.

Frankie 66 This is a perfect supper after a day's racing because, whilst it's light, it's also packed full of strong flavours. 99

39

INSALATA DI PATATINE, ROSMARINO, POMODORINI E OLIVE

Warm salad of sautéed rosemary potatoes with cherry tomatoes and black olives

1 kg waxy potatoes, peeled and cut
into small chunks
extra virgin olive oil
3 tablespoons chopped fresh
rosemary
4 garlic cloves, peeled and left
whole
sea salt and freshly ground black
pepper
12 cherry tomatoes
12 black olives
a handful of chopped fresh flat leaf
parsley

Serves: 4
Preparation time: 15 minutes
Cooking time: 30 minutes

Parboil the potatoes until just tender, then drain well.

Heat a thin layer of olive oil in a large frying pan until very hot then add the potatoes, rosemary and garlic cloves, and season with salt. Turn the potatoes in the oil so everything is well coated, then leave to brown over a low to medium heat for about 20 minutes, turning occasionally so that the potatoes don't burn or stick to the pan.

When the potatoes are golden and a little crunchy on the outside, turn down the heat and throw in the tomatoes and olives, and gently stir. Cook for a few minutes, until the tomatoes start to go a little limp.

To serve, remove the garlic cloves (if you prefer – although I like to keep them in), sprinkle on the parsley and season to taste.

Marco " I love this warm salad on its own with a big glass of something, but it's equally good with any kind of grilled meat or fish, or as an alternative to roast potatoes at Sunday lunch. The secret here is to get your oil really hot before adding the potatoes, so they get nice and crunchy, then turn the heat down a little when adding the tomatoes. "

41

INSALATA AL BALSAMICO

Sautéed Prosciutto di Parma and balsamic vinegar salad

1 cos lettuce, leaves torn off and roughly chopped

a handful of fresh flat leaf parsley leaves

a handful of wild rocket

a handful of escarole or curly endive

a handful of chopped mixed fresh herbs – dill, mint leaves and basil leaves

8 very thin slices of Prosciutto di Parma (Parma ham)

25 g butter

1 tablespoon good balsamic vinegar

1 tablespoon red wine vinegar

5 tablespoons extra virgin olive oil

a pinch of sugar

sea salt

Serves: 4
Preparation time: 10 minutes
Cooking time: 10 minutes

Combine the cos lettuce, parsley, rocket, escarole and mixed herbs in a bowl. Cut the prosciutto into strips and sauté with the butter in a frying pan, until just crisp. Remove from the heat. Add the balsamic and red wine vinegars, olive oil, sugar and a grinding of sea salt. Allow to infuse for 10 minutes. Reheat until tepid, then pour over the salad leaves and serve immediately.

Marco " This wonderful hearty (but healthy) salad is perfect for a light weekend lunch or supper, or as a starter. The secret is to ensure the prosciutto has cooled before you add it to the leaves and to add the dressing at the very last minute. Whilst it is great for the waistline, unfortunately it's especially good with warm ciabatta, which somewhat defeats the object. But you know what they say: 'pane è vita', which roughly translates as 'bread is life'. "

INSALATA DI PISELLI

Fresh green pea salad

600 g fresh peas
6 tablespoons extra virgin olive oil
salt
a handful of skinned whole
   almonds
1 tablespoon chopped fresh flat
   leaf parsley
1 tablespoon chopped fresh
   tarragon

Serves: 4
Preparation time: 5 minutes
Cooking time: 5 minutes

Cook the peas in a pan of salted boiling water for 5 minutes. Drain well and place in a salad bowl. Add the oil and season with a little salt. Leave to cool. Roughly chop the almonds and add to the cooled peas. Mix in the parsley and tarragon, and serve.

Frankie " My dad loves peas; I swear he can eat them at every meal. His favourite dish from my mother's repertoire was Piselli alla Francese (see page 175) but even he got tired of it day in day out, so mum would occasionally make this for a bit of variety. I sometimes like to toast the almonds for a smoky flavour, and the tarragon makes it a great dish to serve with roast chicken. "

43

PASTA
E RISO
PASTA AND RICE

SPAGHETTI CON ARAGOSTA ALL'AMERICANA
Spaghetti with lobster

SPAGHETTI BOLOGNESE

SPAGHETTI ALLA SORRENTINA
Spaghetti with Mozzarella and cherry tomatoes

SPAGHETTI ALLE VONGOLE
Spaghetti with fresh clams

RAVIOLI

GNOCCHI ALLA GENOVESE
Gnocchi with basil, celery
and Pecorino cheese

LASAGNA AL FORNO

SPAGHETTI AL BURRO
Spaghetti with butter

SPAGHETTI AI GAMBERETTI
PICCHI-PACCHI
Spaghetti with tiger prawns

TAGLIOLINI GRATINATI
Tagliolini 'au gratin'

BUCATINI ALLA BOTTARGA
Bucatini pasta with grey mullet roe

TORTELLI DI ERBETTE
Tortellini with spinach leaves

POLENTA CONDITA
Polenta with a rich tomato and mushroom sauce

SUGO DI POMODORI E FUNGHI SECCHI
Tomato sauce with dried mushrooms

RISOTTO ALL'ARAGOSTA
E GAMBERETTI
Lobster and scampi risotto

RISOTTO AGLI SPINACI CON FONTINA
Spinach and Fontina cheese risotto

RISOTTO CON ZUCCA
Risotto with pumpkin

SPAGHETTI CON ARAGOSTA ALL'AMERICANA

Spaghetti with lobster

3 tablespoons extra virgin olive oil
1 onion, finely chopped
1 fresh red chilli pepper, de-seeded
   and finely chopped
1 garlic clove, finely chopped
8 cherry tomatoes, halved
400 g cooked lobster meat tail,
   roughly chopped
100 ml white wine
400 ml lobster bouillion or fish stock
sea salt
700 g dried spaghetti
4 tablespoons chopped fresh flat
   leaf parsley

FOR THE POMODORO SAUCE:

2 onions, finely chopped
1 garlic clove, finely chopped
50 g unsalted butter
2 x 400 g tins of tomatoes
a handful of fresh basil leaves
2 tablespoons caster sugar
sea salt

Serves: 4
Preparation time: 20 minutes
Cooking time: 1 hour

First, make the pomodoro sauce. Fry the onions and garlic in the butter over a medium heat until softened. Then add the tinned tomatoes, basil leaves, sugar and a pinch of salt. Reduce the heat, cover with a lid and simmer for 40 minutes. When cooked, remove the basil leaves and set aside.

Then, heat the olive oil in a saucepan, add the onion, chilli and garlic, cherry tomatoes, lobster tail meat, white wine, fish stock and pomodoro sauce. Cook over a high heat for about 5 minutes until reduced by half. Season to taste.

Meanwhile, bring a large pan of salted water to the boil and cook the spaghetti according to the instructions on the packet. Drain the spaghetti, mix it into the sauce, add the parsley and drizzle over some olive oil. Serve immediately in warmed bowls.

Frankie " What a wonderful way to eat pasta! Catherine makes this when she's feeling a little romantic or just wants to spoil me. Luckily, we have very similar taste in food and we both love lobster. It's important not to swamp the lobster meat in sauce and to eat it as soon as it's ready. There's only one addition needed: chilled champagne and a bit of Frankie in the background ... Sinatra, that is. "

SPAGHETTI BOLOGNESE

700 g dried spaghetti

200 ml pomodoro sauce (see page 51)

80 g unsalted butter

4 tablespoons extra virgin olive oil

2 tablespoons chopped fresh flat leaf parsley

4 tablespoons finely grated Parmesan

FOR THE BOLOGNESE SAUCE:

250 g tinned tomatoes

1 tablespoon tomato purée

½ carrot, finely chopped

½ celery stick, finely chopped

½ red onion, finely chopped

300 g minced beef

100 ml extra virgin olive oil

2 sprigs of rosemary (approx 2.5 cm long)

6 fresh sage leaves

100 ml red wine

sea salt and freshly ground black pepper

Serves: 4
Preparation time: 10 minutes
Cooking time: 1 hour

To make the Bolognese sauce, combine the tinned tomatoes, tomato purée, carrot, celery and red onion in a food processor and pulse until the vegetables are chopped and all the ingredients combined. In a large saucepan, fry the beef in the olive oil for a couple of minutes until lightly browned. Add the tomato and vegetable mixture, the rosemary and sage, the red wine and 200 ml of cold water. Season, stir and bring to the boil. Reduce the heat and simmer for 40 minutes, uncovered. When cooked, remove the rosemary sprigs and sage leaves, and set aside.

Once the Bolognese sauce is cooked, bring a large pan of salted water to the boil and cook the spaghetti according to the instructions on the packet. Then drain and keep warm. Place the pomodoro sauce in a separate saucepan, add the butter and bring it to the boil. Add the Bolognese sauce and the still-warm spaghetti and toss well with the olive oil. To serve, divide between 4 warmed bowls and sprinkle with the chopped parsley and grated Parmesan.

Frankie " This is everyone's favourite pasta dish: a little bit Italian, a little bit American, and a little bit of everywhere else. There are so many versions that it's almost impossible to give a definitive recipe. In Bologna, for example, they have never even heard of it, yet it graces the tables of homes all over the world. Here's my version: I think the fresh herbs make all the difference and, while it's not really 'the done thing' to order this in Italy, I love it. "

SPAGHETTI ALLA SORRENTINA

Spaghetti with Mozzarella and cherry tomatoes

700 g dried spaghetti
150 ml extra virgin olive oil
20 cherry tomatoes, quartered
300 ml pomodoro sauce (see page
  51)
150 g Mozzarella di Bufala
a handful of fresh basil leaves

Serves: 4
Preparation time: 5 minutes
Cooking time: 15 minutes

Cook the spaghetti in a large pan of salted water according to the instructions on the packet, and then drain.

Heat 100 ml of the olive oil in a saucepan, add the quartered cherry tomatoes and fry gently for about a minute. Next add the pomodoro sauce and bring it to the boil.

Mix in the spaghetti, remaining olive oil and Mozzarella, and serve immediately in warmed bowls, topped with torn basil leaves.

Frankie " This is one of my mother's recipes which she would make for my dad on the few occasions he allowed himself a little pasta during the racing season. The sauce is practically raw, with tomatoes that are warmed through with a little Mozzarella, so it makes for a light dish. "

SPAGHETTI ALLE VONGOLE

Spaghetti with fresh clams

700 g spaghetti

150 ml extra virgin olive oil

½ onion, finely chopped

½ clove of garlic, finely chopped

1 small, fresh, red or green chilli,
    finely chopped

1 kg palourdes fresh clams,
    washed and cleaned

100 ml white wine

80 g unsalted butter

2 tablespoons chopped fresh flat
    leaf parsley

FOR THE ANCHOVY PASTE:

3 anchovy fillets, chopped

2 garlic cloves, crushed

1 small shallot, finely chopped

2 tablespoons finely chopped fresh
    flat leaf parsley

3 tablespoons extra virgin olive oil

Serves: 4
Preparation time: 30 minutes
Cooking time: 15 minutes

Mix together all the ingredients for the anchovy paste and set aside. Cook the spaghetti in a large pan of salted boiling water until *al dente*, then drain and keep warm.

In a large saucepan, heat half the olive oil, then add the onion, garlic, chilli, clams and white wine. Cover with a tight-fitting lid and cook over a low heat for about 5 minutes, until all the clams have steamed open.

Drain off and discard half the cooking liquor. Then add the butter and anchovy paste to the remaining liquor, mix in the still-warm spaghetti and toss with the parsley and remainder of the olive oil.

Serve immediately in warmed bowls.

Frankie " This classic dish from southern Italy is popular the world over. Once more, it's all about sourcing the best ingredients. In this case, the clams need to be spanking fresh, so don't be tempted to use the tinned ones. "

57

RAVIOLI

FOR THE STUFFING:

30 g butter

2 shallots, finely chopped

225 g stewing or pie veal, finely diced

3 tablespoons fresh breadcrumbs

2 eggs, beaten

2 tablespoons olive oil

60 g Parmigiano Reggiano, freshly grated

FOR THE PASTA:

450 g strong white plain flour

a pinch of salt

3 large eggs

4–6 tablespoons warm milk

Serves: 4
Preparation time: 1 hour 40 minutes
Cooking time: 2–4 minutes

Start by making the stuffing. Melt the butter in a saucepan and cook the shallots gently for a couple of minutes until soft; don't allow them to colour. Dice the veal and add to the pan. Cook until the meat is light golden brown. Remove from the pan and chop the mixture finely, either by hand or with a food processor. Place in a bowl, add all the remaining ingredients and combine. Knead into a ball and refrigerate whilst you make the pasta or for at least 30 minutes.

Now for the pasta: mix the salt into the flour then tip onto a clean, dry work surface and make a well in the centre. Beat the eggs and carefully and gradually add them to the well, working together with the flour to form a dough. Slowly add the milk as you work the mixture. When the dough is smooth, roll it into a ball and put aside to rest, covered with a tea towel, for 10 minutes.

After it has rested, knead the dough again for 5 to 10 minutes on a floured surface. Divide into two, one piece slightly smaller than the other, and place both balls in a bowl, cover with Clingfilm and leave to rest for at least 15 minutes. The dough is now ready for rolling out.

If you have a pasta machine, use it following the instructions on the machine. If not, do it by hand: remove the larger piece of dough from the bowl leaving the smaller one covered to prevent it drying out. Flour a rolling-pin and your work surface. Place the dough on the work surface and gently roll it out, rotating it from time to time as you do so, so that you have an even round shape. Be careful not to press too hard or the dough will stick to the work surface. Always roll away from your body. Continue until the sheet of dough is about 3 mm thick.

The next stage is slightly more difficult but with practice becomes quite simple. The aim is to stretch the sheet of dough using your hands and the rolling pin; don't use the pin to flatten the dough as you would when making pastry. You should end up with a sheet of dough so thin that it is almost transparent. Wrap the far end of the circle of dough round the rolling pin

and roll the pin back and forth without pressing down on it; at the same time, use the heel of your hands to pull and stretch the dough out from the centre of the pin towards the ends. You will have to repeat this rolling and stretching process quite a few times until the pasta is very, very thin indeed. You will also need to work quickly so that the pasta does not dry out. Leave on the work surface and cover lightly with a slightly damp cloth.

Now do the same with the smaller piece. When you have done this, place little heaps of stuffing (about 1 teaspoonful at a time) in rows approximately 5 cm apart along the length of the sheet.

When you have used up all the stuffing, lay the second, larger sheet of pasta over the top. This sheet will mould itself over the lumps of stuffing so that you can gently spread the pockets out with your fingers, pressing the dough together around the stuffing.

With a pasta cutting wheel, or failing that a very sharp knife, cut between each row of filling, first lengthways and then across so that you end up with little square parcels of pasta. To seal each parcel, gently press round the edges with the back of a fork.

Heat a large pan of salted water. When it is boiling, carefully add the ravioli and cook for 2–4 minutes until they rise to the top and the pasta is tender.

Serve in warmed deep-bottomed bowls, with a tomato sauce or simply drizzled with melted butter and a generous sprinkling of Parmigiano.

Frankie " Ravioli originates from Emilgia Romagna, a part of Italy known for its wonderfully rich food. The local people cook using a lot of butter, cheese and eggs, and this dish is no exception. The ravioli used here are wonderful served with a simple tomato sauce or just with butter and freshly grated Parmesan. "

60

GNOCCHI ALLA GENOVESE

Gnocchi with basil, celery and Pecorino cheese

1 kg King Edward potatoes
100 ml vegetable stock
75 g unsalted butter
180 g Tipo 00 flour (if unavailable,
    plain flour will suffice)
2 eggs
a pinch of nutmeg
sea salt
4 tablespoons finely grated
    Parmesan
4 fresh basil leaves, to garnish

FOR THE GENOVESE SAUCE:
a handful of celery leaves
a handful of fresh basil leaves
a handful of flat leaf parsley leaves
1 tablespoon pine nuts
1 tablespoon grated Pecorino
    cheese
4 tablespoons extra virgin olive oil
a pinch of sea salt

Serves: 4
Preparation time: 50 minutes
Cooking time: 20 minutes

Clean and boil the potatoes in their skins until tender. Peel whilst hot, mash well and set aside to cool.

Combine the Genovese sauce ingredients in a food processor until smooth. In a saucepan, bring the vegetable stock to the boil, whisk in the butter and then add the Genovese sauce. Set aside, keeping warm.

To form the dough for the gnocchi, mix together the cooled potato mash, flour, eggs, nutmeg and salt. On a lightly floured surface, divide the dough into 2 halves and, using a very light touch, roll the dough into a long sausage shape (approximately 1 cm thick and about a metre long). Then cut the dough into 1 cm pieces. When all the dough has been used up, drop the gnocchi into a large pot of boiling salted water for approximately 3 minutes, or until they rise to the surface. To serve, drain the gnocchi, mix in the Genovese sauce, sprinkle over the Parmesan and top with the basil leaves.

Marco " For those of you who have never tried gnocchi 'fatt'in casa', that is to say 'made at home' by a mother or grandmother in the old fashioned way, this dish is an education. My mum made this a lot, so I always think of her when I make it. It's important to keep the dough as light as a feather, so cool hands and a light touch are imperative. Do try to use Tipo 00 flour – authentic Italian pizza flour – if possible. "

LASAGNA AL FORNO

16 fresh lasagna sheets, blanched
   for 3 minutes in boiling water
   and refreshed in cold water
4 tablespoons finely grated
   Parmesan

FOR THE BOLOGNESE SAUCE:

300 g minced beef
100 ml extra virgin olive oil
400 g tinned tomatoes
3 tablespoons tomato purée
½ carrot, roughly chopped
½ celery stick, roughly chopped
½ red onion, chopped
2 sprigs of rosemary (approx 2.5 cm)
6 fresh sage leaves
100 ml red wine
salt and freshly ground black pepper

FOR THE BÉCHAMEL SAUCE:

100 g unsalted butter
100 g plain flour
1 litre milk
a pinch of nutmeg
salt

Preheat the oven to 180°C/350°F/Gas Mark 4.

First, make the Bolognese sauce. In a large saucepan, fry the beef in the olive oil for a couple of minutes until lightly browned. Add the rest of the Bolognese ingredients: the tinned tomatoes, tomato purée, carrot, celery, red onion, rosemary, sage and red wine, and 200 ml of cold water. Season and bring to the boil. Reduce the heat and simmer for 40 minutes, uncovered. When cooked, remove the rosemary sprigs and sage leaves, and set aside.

When the Bolognese sauce is cooked, make the Béchamel sauce. Melt the butter in a saucepan, mix in the flour and cook over a medium heat until the mixture forms a ball that pulls away from the side of the saucepan. Slowly add the milk, whisking continuously, until all the milk is absorbed and it has the consistency of thin cream. Add a grating of nutmeg and a pinch of salt to taste.

In a large ovenproof dish, place alternate layers of first lasagna, then Bolognese and Béchamel sauce, finishing with a layer of Béchamel sauce. Sprinkle with the Parmesan cheese and cook in the oven for 25 minutes. Serve immediately.

Serves: 4
Preparation time: 15 minutes
Cooking time: 65 minutes

Marco " This recipe is so amazing that you'll never buy a ready-made lasagne again. You can use dried pasta, but always cook it first for 3 minutes in boiling salted water with a splash of oil to stop the pasta sticking together. "

SPAGHETTI AL BURRO

Spaghetti with butter

700 g dried spaghetti
200 g Italian or good quality
    unsalted butter
sea salt
4 tablespoons grated Parmesan

Serves: 4
Preparation time: 5 minutes
Cooking time: 10 minutes

Bring a large pan of salted water to the boil, add the spaghetti and cook according to the instructions on the packet. Drain well and return to the pan. Melt the butter in a separate pan and toss with the spaghetti. Season with salt and serve in warmed bowls. Top each serving with a tablespoon of Parmesan.

Marco " This was a great favourite of my mother's. She would pick me up from school to go home for lunch and this was on the menu at least once a week. I adore the taste of the pasta itself, so this butter sauce is perfect. When I make this for me and the kids, I like to eat half a bowl without any Parmesan, just to let the flavour of the spaghetti and butter shine through. I'll then add the cheese at the end. "

SPAGHETTI AI GAMBERETTI PICCHI-PACCHI

Spaghetti with tiger prawns

1 large onion, finely chopped
125 ml extra virgin olive oil
1 large garlic clove, very finely
    chopped
1 large wine glass of good white
    wine
400 g ripe tomatoes, peeled,
    de-seeded and chopped
700 g dried spaghetti
600 g tiger prawns, shelled
a pinch of sugar
salt and freshly ground black
    pepper
a large handful of finely chopped
    fresh flat leaf parsley

Serves: 4
Preparation time: 25 minutes
Cooking time: 55 minutes

Gently fry the onion in the olive oil over a low to medium heat. After about 5 minutes, add the garlic and fry for a further 10 minutes, or until the onions are soft and translucent. Splash in the wine and simmer for 2 or 3 minutes to burn off the alcohol.

Next add the tomatoes and gently cook for 30 minutes to allow the sweetness to permeate the sauce.

Meanwhile, bring a large pan of salted water to the boil and cook the spaghetti according to the packet instructions. Drain well.

Add the prawns to the sauce and simmer for a further 5 minutes until the prawns are cooked through. Add a pinch of sugar, and season to taste. Toss the sauce with the spaghetti, throw in the parsley and serve immediately in warmed bowls.

Frankie " I love the combination of pasta and seafood and have made this dish so many times at home that I've now got it exactly how I like it. There are a lot of prawns in here as one of my pet hates is ordering a seafood pasta in a restaurant and then having to play 'find the prawn'! 'Picchi-pacchi' means a lightly cooked fresh tomato sauce. The name comes from the sound of the fresh tomatoes being squashed against the side of the pot. For extra pizzazz, add half a small red chilli, finely chopped, with the onion and garlic. "

TAGLIOLINI GRATINATI

Tagliolini 'au gratin'

½ onion, chopped
200 g butter
1 sprig of sage
200 g flour
a pinch of nutmeg
1 litre vegetable stock
salt
600g fresh tagliolini
200 ml double cream, whipped
2 egg yolks
120 g Parma ham, cut into fine
  strips
a pinch of paprika
30 ml olive oil
60 g finely grated Parmesan

Serves: 4
Preparation time: 40 minutes
Cooking time: 20 minutes

In a heavy-based pan, cook the onion in the butter with the sage until it softens. Then add the flour and cook for 2–3 minutes. Add the nutmeg then slowly add the vegetable stock, stirring continuously to make a smooth sauce. Season with salt and pass through a fine sieve. Set aside to cool slightly.

Meanwhile, put the pasta into a saucepan of salted boiling water. Bring back to the boil, then turn down the heat so that the pasta simmers to cook. In a bowl, whip the double cream until it thickens to soft peaks then fold in the egg yolks, adding 200 ml of your prepared velouté.

In a saucepan, gently fry the Parma ham and paprika in the olive oil for two minutes and then add the remaining 800 ml of velouté. Add the pasta and mix together thoroughly. Divide between 4 bowls and then spoon over the glazage. Sprinkle over the Parmesan and glaze under a hot grill until golden brown.

Frankie

" This recipe is adapted from the world famous Cipriani restaurant in Venice. It's the most sublime and wonderful dish you'll ever eat. If you really want to make it special, top with shavings of freshly grated truffle. "

69

BUCATINI ALLA BOTTARGA

Bucatini pasta with grey mullet roe

700 g Bucatini pasta
50 g Bottarga, shaved into flakes
extra virgin olive oil
1 garlic clove, finely chopped
a large handful of fresh flat leaf
    parsley, finely chopped
1 fresh red chilli, de-seeded and
    finely chopped
8 fresh basil leaves

Serves: 4
Preparation time: 15 minutes
Cooking time: 10 minutes

Cook the pasta in plenty of boiling, salted water according to the instructions on the packet. Meanwhile, soften the flakes of Bottarga in a little warmed olive oil. In a separate pan, heat 6 tablespoons of olive oil and gently cook the garlic and parsley for a few minutes. Then stir in the Bottarga and chilli and cook for a few seconds. Drain the cooked pasta and add it to the sauce. Serve immediately in warmed bowls, topped with shredded basil leaves.

Frankie " Bottarga is a Sardinian delicacy, made from the dried roe of the grey mullet and pressed into sausage shaped slabs. Here, it is used as a dressing for pasta but it's also delicious eaten raw, thinly shaved and dressed with olive oil and lemon. This was another favourite recipe from my grandmother who treated the delicate flavours of Bottarga with respect and used it sparingly – although a little does go a long way. If you can't find Bucatini pasta, spaghetti will also work well. "

TORTELLI DI ERBETTE

Tortellini with spinach leaves

450 g Tipo 00 flour
4 free range organic eggs, lightly
 beaten, plus 1 extra for sealing
 the tortellini
1 teaspoon salt
150 g melted butter, to serve
lots of grated Parmigiano, to serve

FOR THE FILLING:

170 g very fresh ricotta
170 g cooked green leaves,
 preferably spinach, beet
 or chard, well drained
50 g grated Parmigiano
grated nutmeg
2 eggs, lightly beaten
salt and freshly ground black pepper

Serves: 4
Preparation time: 1 hour
Cooking time: 5 minutes

Pour the flour in a mound onto a table, make a hole in the middle and pour in the eggs and the salt and combine and knead until you have a soft dough. Divide this into 3 pieces. Roll each piece out, stretching and rolling until it is very thin.

To make the 'ripieno' (filling) mix together the ricotta, green leaves, Parmigiano cheese, nutmeg, eggs and salt and pepper to taste.

Cut the rolled out pasta into 5 cm squares, place a small teaspoon of 'ripieno' on one half of the square and cover with the other half, pressing the edges down firmly. Moisten with a little beaten egg so they are firmly closed and won't open during cooking. Repeat the process until all of the 'ripieno' is used up.

Cook the tortellini in plenty of boiling salted water for 4 minutes, until they rise to the top. Serve in a heated tureen with lots of melted butter and plenty of grated Parmigiano.

Marco " One of the great pasta dishes of all time; simple and light but, when made well, nothing can touch it. The secret is using a light touch with cool hands when making the pasta. My great grandmother made this dish at least three times a week with the leaves of young beets from her own garden. Nutmeg is also an essential ingredient and the ricotta should be super fresh and firm to the touch. "

POLENTA CONDITA

Polenta with a rich tomato and mushroom sauce

9 cups of water
1 tablespoon salt
3 cups medium-grind Italian
   polenta or cornmeal

Serves: 4
Preparation time: 5 minutes
Cooking time: 35 minutes

Put the water into a large and heavy-bottomed saucepan and bring it to the boil. Add the salt, lower the heat to medium and gradually add the polenta by sprinkling into the water from your hand, stirring the mixture constantly with a long handled wooden spoon. Take care and be patient as you add the polenta or it will get lumpy.

Continue to stir and cook the mixture constantly; if a lump does appear crush it against the side of the pot with your spoon. You need to stir the polenta for about 30 minutes to get a truly thick, smooth purée. When done it will form large bubbles and pull away from the side of the pot.

If you are serving the polenta soft, with calves' liver for example, it is now ready to eat. If on the other hand you are serving it 'condita', as in this recipe, turn it out onto a board and, using either your hands or a spatula, smooth the polenta. It should be about 7–10 cm thick. After about 10 minutes the polenta will cool fairly rapidly and become firm enough to cut. It can be made the day before you need it and kept in the fridge.

Frankie " The polenta we eat at home in Italy is quite different from the way it is served in restaurants in Britain. My favourite way to cook it is to layer the slices of polenta with a rich mushroom and tomato sauce and then bake it in the oven. It's another one of those traditional Italian dishes that my grandmother made for the whole family and was loved by all. "

SUGO DI POMODORI E FUNGHI SECCHI

Tomato sauce with dried mushrooms

30 g dried porcini mushrooms
30 g butter
3 tablespoons extra virgin olive oil
1 medium onion, finely chopped
400 g tinned Italian plum tomatoes
Sea salt and freshly ground black
  pepper
50 g finely grated Parmigiano

Serves: 4
Preparation time: 40 minutes
Cooking time: 1 hour 20 minutes

Preheat the oven to 180°C/350°F/Gas Mark 4.

Soak the mushrooms in a bowl of hot water for 20–30 minutes. Melt the butter and olive oil in a saucepan over a medium heat and add the onion. Cook over a low heat for 5–7 minutes until the onion is soft – do not allow it to brown. Drain the mushrooms through a sieve lined with kitchen paper, retaining the water the mushrooms were soaked in. Roughly chop the mushrooms, add to the onions and cook for 2–3 minutes. Pass the tinned tomatoes through a sieve over the onion and mushroom mixture. Season to taste and bring to the boil, then turn down the heat and simmer gently for 40 minutes. Add the liquid the mushrooms were soaked in, bring back to the boil then simmer for a further 10 minutes.

To assemble the polenta, put a little of the tomato and mushroom sauce at the bottom of a glass baking dish. Cut slices of polenta to fit the length of the dish about ½–¾ cm thick. Place a layer of polenta slices over the sauce and top with more sauce and a sprinkling of Parmigiano. Keep layering the polenta and sauce until both are finished. The last layer should be the sauce and a large handful of Parmigiano. Bake in the oven for 30 minutes.

Frankie " If you made this dish in Italy you would invariably have gathered the mushrooms yourself. Italians are obsessed with picking mushrooms in September. When the season starts every forest and meadow in Italy is combed for fairy rings which are, of course, where mushrooms grow. The first batch is always fried and any others are then dried and used throughout the year to make sauces such as this. "

RISOTTO ALL'ARAGOSTA E GAMBERETTI

Lobster and scampi risotto

1 lobster, pre-cooked
1 litre stock (preferably the drained
    liquid in which the lobster was
    cooked but failing that a light
    chicken stock)
75 g butter
1 medium onion, very finely
    chopped
350 g Arborio rice
a large glass of dry white wine
50 g grated Parmigiano cheese
a few strands of saffron
50 g butter
16 fresh scampi (Dublin Bay
    prawns, shelled)
salt and freshly ground black
    pepper
juice of a lemon
a wine glass of cognac
flat leaf parsley, finely chopped

Serves: 4
Preparation time: 20 minutes
Cooking time: 30 minutes

Remove all the meat from the lobster, slice it and set aside. Place the stock in a saucepan and bring to the boil, lower the heat and keep it at a gentle simmer. Melt the first 75 g of butter in a large, heavy-bottomed pan and sauté the onion very gently until soft and transparent.

Add the rice and cook, stirring, for about 5 minutes until the rice becomes slightly translucent. Add the wine and, over a medium heat, stir constantly until the alcohol has evaporated and the rice has absorbed all the wine. Add the hot stock gradually, ladle by ladle, stirring the risotto gently all the time for about 20 minutes or until the rice is just tender. It should have a moist, creamy consistency but retain its bite. Add the grated Parmigiano and the saffron and cover to keep warm.

Heat the remaining 50 g of butter in a frying pan and quickly sauté the scampi and lobster. Season with salt, pepper and lemon juice, then add the cognac and cook gently until the alcohol has evaporated.

To serve, divide the risotto between 4 deep plates, top with the lobster and scampi, spooning the juices from the pan over the top, and sprinkle with the chopped parsley.

Frankie " When I want to spoil my wife Catherine and make her feel a little special, I make this risotto. It's such a gorgeous combination of flavours, and cooking someone lobster is a real treat. There's no two ways about it: the only thing to drink with this is champagne – the best you can afford and well chilled. "

RISOTTO AGLI SPINACI CON FONTINA

Spinach and Fontina cheese risotto

1 litre chicken stock
75 g butter
1 medium onion, finely chopped
350 g Arborio or risotto rice
1 small wine glass of dry white
    wine
300 g baby spinach leaves,
    roughly torn
50 g grated Parmesan
a small pinch of freshly grated
    nutmeg
sea salt (optional)
200 g Fontina cheese, cubed

Serves: 4
Preparation time: 5 minutes
Cooking time: 30 minutes

Place the stock in a saucepan, bring it to the boil, then lower the heat and keep it at a gentle simmer.

Melt the butter in a large heavy-bottomed pan, add the onion and fry over a low to medium heat until soft and transparent. Add the rice and stir for about 5 minutes until the rice is slightly translucent. Then increase the heat to medium, add the wine and stir constantly for 2–3 minutes until the rice has absorbed all of the wine. Then gradually stir in the hot stock, ladle by ladle (this should take approximately 20 minutes) until the rice is just tender. It should have a moist, creamy consistency but retain its bite. Halfway through adding the stock, gradually stir in the spinach leaves. When the rice is cooked, add the Parmesan and sprinkle on the nutmeg. Season with salt (if required) and then finally stir in the cubes of Fontina cheese. Serve in deep bowls. The Fontina should be melting and oozing as it reaches the table.

Marco " My kids don't particularly like to eat green, leafy vegetables on their own so this risotto is a winner. Fontina cheese is a creamy Italian mountain cheese and gives this dish a lovely melting consistency. I add an extra handful of spinach and keep the wine in as the alcohol evaporates during the cooking process – I want my children to recognize the true flavours of good food and not a watered-down kiddies' version. "

RISOTTO CON ZUCCA

Risotto with pumpkin

1.5 litres chicken stock
300 g cubed pumpkin flesh
125 ml butter
1 small onion, finely chopped
350 g Arborio or risotto rice
1 wine glass of dry white wine
½ teaspoon powdered saffron or
  2 saffron strands
2 good handfuls of grated
  Parmesan
sea salt and freshly ground black
  pepper

Serves: 4
Preparation time: 10 minutes
Cooking time: 1 hour

Preheat the oven to 180°C/350°F/Gas Mark 4. Bring the chicken stock to preboil and gently simmer.

Wrap the pumpkin cubes in foil, place them in the oven and cook for about 30 minutes until very soft. Then purée in a food processor.

Over a low to medium heat, warm half the butter in a saucepan and gently sauté the onion for a few minutes until soft and translucent. Add the rice and stir for a couple of minutes, then add the wine and cook for a further 2–3 minutes to allow the alcohol to evaporate. Add the pumpkin and enough stock to cover the rice. As the stock reduces, gradually add more, stirring all the time, until the rice is tender but still has a little bite. (This will take about 10 minutes.) Halfway through adding the stock, stir in the saffron. When the rice is cooked, remove from the heat, add the remaining butter and half the Parmesan, cover and allow to sit for a couple of minutes. To serve, place in deep bowls, top with the remaining Parmesan and season to taste.

Marco " This is a recipe my mother cooked for us on cold winter days. When we got home from school, the chicken stock would be bubbling away on the stove and the house would be enveloped in a lovely warm fug. Whilst mum stirred and stirred her risotto, I would sit at the kitchen table and draw pictures for her. The addition of pumpkin gives a wonderful sweet, nutty flavour; you can actually feel it doing you good as you eat it. "

CARNE

MEA

BOLLITO MISTO CON SALSA VERDE
Meat medley with green salsa

SALSA VERDE
Green salsa

SCALLOPPINE DI POLLO CON ERBE
Escalope of chicken with herbs

FRANKIE'S BURGER

SCALLOPPINE DI VITELLO ALLA MILANESE
Escalope of veal alla Milanese

AGNELLO IN PADELLA
CON MELANZANE ARROSTO
Pan fried lamb with roasted aubergine

BISTECCA AL ROSMARINO
Rib eye steak with rosemary,
salt crystal and Béarnaise sauce

BISTECCA FIORENTINA ALLA ROMANA
Rib eye steak alla Romana

ANITRA CON OLIVE
Confit of crispy duck with olives

PANCIA DI MAIALE CON RAGÚ
Honey roast belly pork Marco Polo
with a ragu of cannellini beans

CONIGLIO ALLA CACCIATORA

Hunter's rabbit

POLLO AROMATICO IN CASSERUOLA

Pot roasted chicken with herbs

VITELLO ARROSTO

Roast veal

POLPETTE DI CARNE

Italian meatballs

POLLO AI PEPERONI

Chicken with peppers

BISTECCA ALLA PIZZAIOLA

Steak with garlic, oregano
and tomatoes

ARISTA DI MAIALE AL FINOCCHIO

Roast pork with fennel

AGNELLO AL FORNO

Oven-cooked lamb

BOLLITO MISTO CON SALSA VERDE

Meat medley with green salsa

800 g leg of beef
800 g veal shoulder or breast
1 x 2.5 kg free-range chicken
2 carrots, roughly chopped
2 celery sticks, roughly chopped
2 medium onions, roughly chopped
salt
1 kg Cottechino, Zampone or
    Italian sausages (available from
    all good Italian delicatessens)

Serves: 8
Preparation time: 5 minutes
Cooking time: 2 ¾ hours

Place the beef, veal and chicken in a very large pan of boiling water and cook for a few minutes, until a thick scum forms on the surface. Then drain and rinse the meat. (This will ensure a clearer broth.)

Fill a large pot with cold water, add the carrots, celery, onions and a little salt and bring to the boil. Then add the beef and reduce the heat to a simmer. An hour later, add the veal and chicken, bring it back to the boil, then reduce the heat and simmer for a further 90 minutes, or until the meat is tender, frequently skimming off any impurities from the broth.

Fill another smaller pot with cold water, bring it to the boil, then add the sausages, reduce the heat and simmer gently until cooked through (about 30 minutes, depending on the size of the sausages).

To serve, drain and reserve the broth from the meat and vegetables. Drain the sausages and discard the cooking liquid. Place the meats and sausages on a large, warmed serving platter, top with 2 or 3 ladles of the reserved broth and carve at the table. Serve with a salsa verde (see opposite), floury boiled potatoes, baby carrots and any green vegetable you like.

Marco " This wonderful dish is perfect for the kind of family eating that the Italians do so well. Serve the various meats in the middle of the table and carve as you need them. The salsa verde is my good friend's very special family recipe, passed down from her grandmother, Mary Ghirardani. It is important to boil the water before placing the meat in the pot as it helps to retain its juices and keeps the meat moist. "

SALSA VERDE

Green salsa

125 ml extra virgin olive oil
125 g butter
5 garlic cloves, very finely chopped
4 large handfuls of very finely
  chopped fresh flat leaf parsley,
  stalks removed
4 tablespoons tomato purée,
  dissolved in 3 tablespoons hot
  water
freshly ground sea salt
a pinch of nutmeg
8 tablespoons white wine vinegar
4 tablespoons white sugar
2 hard boiled eggs
1 teaspoon white wine vinegar

Makes: 600 ml
Preparation time: 15 minutes
Cooking time: 10 minutes

Place the olive oil and butter in a saucepan and heat gently until the butter has melted. Add the garlic and parsley and fry over a very low heat until the garlic has softened (but don't let it brown). Add the tomato purée and season with the salt and nutmeg. Then add the white wine vinegar and sugar, and cook over a very low heat, until the sugar has dissolved. Remove from the heat and set aside until it has cooled to room temperature.

Extract the yolks from the hard boiled eggs and place them in a small bowl with 1 teaspoon of white wine vinegar. Mix together to form a paste. Chop the white of the eggs very finely and mix it into the salsa with the egg yolk paste. Place the salsa in a glass jar with a lid and store in the fridge until ready to use.

Serve the salsa at room temperature or warmed over a low heat.

$\mathcal{M}$arco " This sauce is perfect with Bollito Misto, as well as with almost any roasted or grilled meat. I love it with roast chicken on a Sunday and, even more so, with cold chicken salad sandwiches the day after. Try it as part of an antipasto or even just as a dip with some crusty bread and a glass of wine. It will keep for up to three days in the refrigerator. "

SCALLOPPINE DI POLLO CON ERBE

Escalope of chicken with herbs

4 organic skinless chicken breasts
1 teaspoon chopped fresh flat leaf
   parsley
1 teaspoon chopped tarragon
1 teaspoon chopped chervil
2 lemons, halved, to garnish
sea salt

FOR THE SALAD:

1 handful of baby spinach leaves
1 handful of wild rocket
1 handful picked watercress
1 tablespoon fresh flat leaf parsley
1 tablespoon fresh chervil
1 tablespoon chopped fresh
   tarragon
1 tablespoon sage leaves

FOR THE DRESSING:

2 tablespoons white wine vinegar
1 teaspoon mayonnaise
sea salt
a pinch of sugar
6 tablespoons extra virgin olive oil

Serves: 4
Preparation time: 15 minutes
Cooking time: 15 minutes

For the dressing, put the vinegar, mayonnaise, salt and sugar in a bowl and mix together. Then slowly trickle in the olive oil, stirring all the time, until the mixture has emulsified

Butterfly the chicken breasts by slicing them horizontally until they are almost cut in half and then open them out. Beat out thinly with a meat mallet until they are about 1 cm thick. Place the chicken on a hot grill/griddle pan that has been brushed with a little olive oil. Sprinkle over the chopped parsley, tarragon and chervil and cook for approximately 2 minutes on each side until cooked through. Toss the salad ingredients with the dressing and divide between 4 plates. Add the chicken, garnish with the halved lemons and sprinkle with sea salt.

Marco "This is one of my mother's recipes from her home town near Genoa which she adapted when she moved to England. At home she would have used veal but in the 1960s veal was hard to come by in Manchester so she used an escalope of chicken cut from the breast which worked just as well. It's a very simple dish but the herbs and lemon are just perfect with the meat. Using sea salt is really important here as it makes the flavours sing through. "

FRANKIE'S BURGER

1 onion, very finely chopped
8 slices of smoked back bacon
800 g organic Aberdeen Angus
   rump steak, minced
sea salt and freshly ground black
   pepper
4 tablespoons olive oil
4 hamburger buns
4 slices of cheese of your choice

Serves: 4
Preparation time: 10 minutes
Cooking time: 7 minutes

Gently fry the onion until softened and then leave to cool. Grill the bacon until crispy and keep warm. Combine the onion with the minced meat, season with salt and pepper and then divide the mixture to form 4 burgers, approximately 2 cm thick. Brush the burgers with a little olive oil and cook under a very hot grill for approximately 3 minutes on each side, or to your liking. Allow to rest for 5 minutes. To serve, toast the hamburger buns on the cut side only. Place the burger, the cheese slices, then the bacon in the bun. Serve with tomato ketchup or mayonnaise.

Frankie " I know this isn't exactly Italian peasant cuisine but, frankly, there are times when nothing on earth can beat the pure, gluttonous satisfaction of a really good burger. Everyone eats their burger differently – I like to cut it in half and eat it with my hands, while slurping on a nice glass of red. Trashy perhaps but molto buono! "

SCALLOPPINE DI VITELLO ALLA MILANESE

Escalope of veal alla Milanese

4 veal escalopes (approximately
   150 g each)
200 g plain flour
6 whole eggs, beaten
200 g fresh breadcrumbs
100 ml olive oil
4 handfuls of cherry tomatoes on
   the vine, grilled until slightly soft
sea salt
2 lemons, halved, to garnish

Serves: 4
Preparation time: 20 minutes
Cooking time: 10 minutes

Dip each escalope into the flour, the egg and then the breadcrumbs, until both sides are well covered. Heat the olive oil in a frying pan, allow the oil to sizzle and then add the escalopes, and fry for a couple of minutes on each side until golden. (You will probably need to do 2 at a time to avoid overcrowding the pan.) To serve, place an escalope on each plate, lay the cherry tomatoes on top, sprinkle with sea salt and garnish with half a lemon.

Frankie " 'Cotoletta' is the traditional name for this dish. It's served to thousands of kids every day on their return from school all over Italy and I was no exception. It's a bit like today's chicken nuggets except it's cooked with olive oil, made with one hundred per cent meat and served with salad, so it's much healthier! I give it to my kids all the time and they love it. "

AGNELLO IN PADELLA
CON MELANZANE ARROSTO

Pan fried lamb with roasted aubergine

4 medium sized aubergines
4 garlic cloves
a large sprig of fresh rosemary cut
    into about eight 2 cm pieces
150 ml extra virgin olive oil
4 shallots, very finely chopped
1 tablespoon tomato pureé
salt and freshly ground black
    pepper
4 pieces of lamb fillet, weighing
    200 g each
150 ml red wine
a pinch of sugar

Serves: 4
Preparation time: 30 minutes
Cooking time: 45 minutes

Preheat the oven to 200°C/400°F/Gas Mark 6. Halve the aubergines lengthways and score the flesh almost to the bottom without breaking the skin, first one way then another at an angle to give a diamond pattern. Slice the garlic and dot around between the cuts, then do the same with the rosemary. Put the halves back together again so that you once more have 4 whole aubergines, wrap in foil and place on a roasting tray in the oven for 30 minutes.

When the aubergines are cooked remove the foil and the garlic and rosemary and spoon out the flesh into a colander. Leave over a bowl to cool and drain. When cooled, chop the flesh very finely.

Heat 4 tablespoons of oil in a saucepan, add the shallots and cook gently for 4–5 minutes until softened (do not allow them to colour). Then add the chopped aubergine and the tomato purée and cook gently until all the moisture from the aubergine has evaporated. Season with salt and pepper.

Season the lamb fillets, heat a little oil in a frying pan until very hot and brown the fillets on both sides for 2–3 minutes, depending on the thickness of the meat. The lamb should be served pink. Take off the heat and rest the meat for at least 5 minutes. Deglaze the pan with the red wine, boiling rapidly to reduce it by half. Add a pinch of sugar. Check the seasoning.

Reheat the aubergine and place a spoonful in the centre of 4 warmed dinner plates, slice the lamb on a slant and lay the slices at an angle around the aubergine. Finally, drizzle the whole thing with a little of the pan juices.

$Marco$ " Italians don't really eat a lot of lamb and this dish appeared on our table once my mother had settled in England and her cooking had acquired a touch of the Italo/Inglese, a combination of Italian method with English ingredients. The aubergine adds the Mediterranean touch, as of course do the wonderful array of fresh herbs. Sauté potatoes go perfectly with this dish. "

95

BISTECCA AL ROSMARINO

Rib eye steak with rosemary, salt crystal and Béarnaise sauce

100 ml extra virgin olive oil
4 rosemary sprigs (approximately
    10 cm in length)
4 Aberdeen Angus rib eye steaks
    (approximately 275 g each)
sea salt

FOR THE BÉARNAISE SAUCE:

2 shallots, finely chopped
6 tablespoons tarragon vinegar
    (you can use 2 sprigs of tarragon
    and white wine vinegar as an
    alternative)
6 whole black peppercorns
3 bunches of fresh tarragon, stalks
    discarded and finely chopped
4 egg yolks
2 teaspoons Dijon mustard
300 g butter, softened and cubed
salt

Serves: 4
Preparation time: 20 minutes
Cooking time: 6 minutes

To make the Béarnaise sauce, put the shallots in a saucepan and add the vinegar, peppercorns and tarragon. Bring to the boil and cook for 1 or 2 minutes until reduced by half. Strain the liquid through a sieve and set aside. In a glass bowl, whisk together the egg yolks and mustard. Then place the bowl over a saucepan of gently simmering water. Whisk in the reduced vinegar mixture, reduce the heat, and then gradually add the butter one cube at a time, whisking constantly until the sauce is thick and velvety. (You may need to turn the heat off while adding the butter as the sauce must not bubble.) Once all the butter has been incorporated, season with a little salt. (To keep the sauce warm, cover it with a clean tea towel and leave to sit over a pan of hot water with the heat off, whisking from time to time.)

Before cooking the steaks, heat the olive oil in a small saucepan and gently fry the rosemary sprigs for a few minutes over a medium heat until crispy. Take out the rosemary sprigs and keep to one side, and allow the remaining oil to cool in the pan. Place the steaks on a very hot grill/griddle pan that has been brushed with olive oil and grill to your liking. (For a medium-cooked steak, grill each side for approximately 3 minutes.) Top each steak with a crispy rosemary sprig, drizzle on the cooled rosemary oil, add a sprinkling of salt crystals and serve with the Béarnaise sauce in a jug on the side.

Marco "The true Florentine rib eye steak is huge, similar to an American T-bone, and is always from a young cow. Rib eye is my favourite cut as it has a lot of flavour, due to the high proportion of fat marbled through the meat. I like to cook my steak simply and serve it with a simple salad and good bread, and a rich Béarnaise sauce on the side. "

BISTECCA FIORENTINA ALLA ROMANA

Rib eye steak alla Romana

100 ml extra virgin olive oil
400 g tin of cooked snails, drained
4 Aberdeen Angus or good quality
    Italian rib eye steaks
    (approximately 280 g each)
sea salt

FOR THE GARLIC BUTTER:

100 g unsalted butter
3 garlic cloves, crushed
1 tablespoon chopped fresh flat
    leaf parsley
salt

Serves: 4
Preparation time: 20 minutes
Cooking time: 7 minutes

Mix together all the garlic butter ingredients, and then place with the olive oil in a pan on a low heat. Add the snails and warm gently (do not let the sauce bubble). Place the steaks on a very hot grill that has been brushed with olive oil and cook to your liking (or for approximately 3 minutes on each side for a medium-cooked steak). To serve, place the snails over each steak, pour on the buttery juices and sprinkle with sea salt.

Marco " This is the Italian equivalent of 'surf and turf'. It's very much a hunter's dish and extremely popular at Frankie's "

ANITRA CON OLIVE

Confit of crispy duck with olives

4 large legs of organic duck (each approximately 300–400 g with bone)

2 litres tinned duck fat, at room temperature

1 whole garlic bulb, halved

10 whole black peppercorns

1 bay leaf

4 sprigs of fresh thyme

100 ml extra virgin olive oil

16 black olives, stoned and halved

sea salt

FOR THE MARINADE:

200 g rock salt

1 teaspoon chopped fresh thyme leaves

6 garlic cloves, crushed

Serves: 4
Preparation time: 20 minutes
Cooking time: 3 hours 20 minutes
Marinating time: 6 hours
Cooling time: 1 hour

Preheat the oven to 170°C/325°F/Gas Mark 3.

Mix together the marinade ingredients and rub into the duck legs. Cover and leave to stand for 6 hours. Then wash off the marinade, dry the legs thoroughly with kitchen paper and place on a large baking tray. Pour the duck fat over the legs, add the halved garlic bulb, peppercorns, bay leaf and sprigs of thyme and place in the oven for 45 minutes. Then lower the oven temperature to 130°C/250°F/Gas Mark ½ and cook for 2½ hours. Remove from the oven and leave to cool.

When the duck legs have cooled, put the olive oil and black olives in a saucepan and warm over a low heat, until tepid. Meanwhile, place the duck legs in a heated, lightly-oiled frying pan, skin-side down, and place in the oven at 220°C/425°F/Gas Mark 7 for approximately 7 minutes, until crisp and golden brown. To serve, place the duck legs on a plate, spoon over the warmed olives and olive oil, and sprinkle with sea salt.

Marco " Duck isn't so popular in Italy but, during my childhood, it was often on the table after days out hunting with my dad. This is his recipe and I was really excited about putting it on the menu at Frankie's as I remember how grown up I felt eating the food that I had bagged. "

PANCIA DI MAIALE CON RAGÚ

Honey roast belly pork Marco Polo with a ragu of cannellini beans

1.5 kg organic pork belly
a handful of rock salt
4 sprigs of thyme
10 black peppercorns
1 bay leaf
1 whole garlic bulb, halved
2 litres duck fat
125 g dried cannellini beans,
    soaked overnight
150 ml extra virgin olive oil

FOR THE MARCO POLO GLAZE:

7 tablespoons clear honey
1 teaspoon crushed coriander
    seeds

Serves: 4
Preparation time: 20 minutes
Cooking time: 6 hours

Preheat the oven to 130°C/250°F/Gas Mark ½.

Place the pork belly in a deep-sided roasting dish, season with the rock salt and add the thyme, peppercorns, bay leaf and garlic halves. Then cover well with the duck fat, place in the oven and cook for 6 hours without a lid.

For the glaze, put the honey in a saucepan and cook over a medium heat, until it is reduced by half. Then mix in the crushed coriander seeds.

Place the soaked cannellini beans in a heavy-bottomed pan, cover with cold water, bring to the boil, then drain and refresh under a cold running tap. Warm the cannellini beans in olive oil until tepid.

Take the pork belly out of the oven, remove it from the duck fat and leave to cool. When cooled, cut the pork into 4 rectangles, and then cut away the fat from the top of each rectangle to make the crackling. Thinly slice the fat, place it under a hot grill and cook until it is crispy.

Preheat the oven to 180°C/350°F/Gas Mark 4. Brush the pork with the Marco Polo glaze and place in the oven for approximately 5 minutes. To serve, place a large spoonful of the cannellini beans in the centre of a soup plate, and top with the glazed pork belly and still-warm crackling.

Frankie “ This dish ranks high on my Foodie Wish List – that is the food I wish I could eat from time to time without having to constantly worry about my racing weight. It tastes so good that sometimes I can't resist! ”

CONIGLIO ALLA CACCIATORA

Hunter's rabbit

1 rabbit, approx 2.5 kg (preferably
  wild), cut into 12 portions by
  your butcher
sea salt and freshly ground pepper
plain flour
3 tablespoons extra virgin olive oil
1 onion, chopped
1 carrot, chopped
2 celery sticks, chopped
2 garlic cloves, crushed and
  chopped
2 large handfuls of fresh flat leaf
  parsley, finely chopped
1 wine glass of white wine
1 x 400 g tin of chopped tomatoes
200 g black olives, stoned

Serves: 4
Preparation time: 10 minutes
Cooking time: 1 hour 20 minutes

Preheat the oven to 180°C/350°F/Gas Mark 4.

Season the rabbit portions with salt and pepper, coat with plain flour, and then fry in the olive oil for a few minutes until lightly browned all over.

In a large ovenproof casserole dish, gently fry the onion, carrot, celery, garlic and parsley in 6 tablespoons of the olive oil. When the onion is soft and just beginning to colour, add the rabbit joints, chopped liver and white wine, and then boil rapidly for a few minutes to burn off the alcohol.

Add the tomatoes, olives and 1 tablespoon of plain flour, and then cover and cook in the oven for 1 hour. Check every 20 minutes and add a little stock (whatever you have to hand) or water, if it gets a bit dry.

Serve with mashed potato or polenta.

Marco " Rabbit is a vastly underrated meat with lots of flavour and a low fat content, and this is a great dish to cook with it. As a young boy, I hunted wild rabbits with my father. Now, as then, I kill to eat, not for fun. Everything I shoot ends up on my table and I firmly believe that a good cook needs to understand the food they are preparing and where it has come from. This recipe is dedicated to all fellow hunter-gatherers out there. "

POLLO AROMATICO IN CASSERUOLA

Pot roasted chicken with herbs

1 large (approx 2 kg) organic
   chicken, cut into 6–8 pieces
6 tablespoons extra virgin olive oil
3 garlic cloves, peeled and roughly
   chopped
2 small onions, quartered
3 sprigs of fresh rosemary
2 bay leaves
1 sprig of fresh thyme
200 ml dry white wine
salt and freshly ground black
   pepper

Serves: 4
Preparation time: 5 minutes
Cooking time: 45 minutes

Wash and pat the chicken dry, inside and out. Trim off any excess fat, keeping the skin on.

Over a low heat, warm the olive oil in a large heavy-bottomed saucepan, add the garlic and onion and fry for a few minutes to flavour the oil. Add the chicken and brown on both sides, starting skin-side down. Add the rosemary, bay leaves, thyme and white wine, and boil rapidly for a couple of minutes until the alcohol has evaporated.

Lower the heat, cover with a tight-fitting lid and cook for 30 minutes, checking occasionally to ensure the chicken is well basted. The wine and juices from the bird should form a wonderfully aromatic gravy.

To serve, remove any woody sprigs of herbs, place the chicken pieces on a large serving plate and top with the juices from the meat.

Frankie **"** This dish reminds me of hot summer Sundays spent on my grandparents' farm. We kids would be frogmarched to the local village church while my grandmother got to stay home and cook – methinks she got the better deal! The smell of chicken, rosemary and garlic was heavenly and filled the house with a sense of well-being. My grandfather would kill the chicken the night before as he felt it was morally wrong to do so on a Sunday! **"**

VITELLO ARROSTO

Roast veal

4 tablespoons extra virgin olive oil
800 g piece rump of veal
sea salt and freshly ground pepper
200 g pancetta, finely chopped
1 clove garlic
4 sage leaves
a sprig of rosemary
4 sprigs of parsley
1 bay leaf
large glass of white wine
50 g butter

Serves: 4
Preparation time: 10 minutes
Cooking time: 1½ hours

Preheat the oven to 180°C/350°F/Gas Mark 4.

Heat the olive oil in a large, heavy-bottomed saucepan. Season the meat with salt and pepper and brown on all sides. Remove the meat from the pan and set aside.

Add the pancetta, garlic and herbs to the pan, allow to soften slightly then turn up the heat, add the wine and allow the alcohol to evaporate. Put the veal back into the pan and place in the oven for an hour and a half, basting every now and then with the juices from the pan. Towards the end of cooking, baste the veal with the butter.

To serve, remove the woody parts of the herbs and the bay leaf and carve into 1 cm slices.

Frankie " Roast veal is extremely popular in Italy, and this is one of the nicest ways to prepare it. This recipe is my mother's and was served only on special occasions, high days and holidays. The meat is served simply with a light 'sugo' made entirely from its natural juices. Whilst I love to eat it straight from the oven, it's also really good the day after served cold in a sandwich with a little Salsa Verde (see page 87). "

108

POLPETTE DI CARNE

Italian meatballs

225 g fresh white breadcrumbs
1 cup of milk
450 g rump steak, finely chopped
    or ground
¼ cup of freshly grated Parmigiano
2 large eggs
handful of chopped flat leaf parsley
salt and freshly ground black
    pepper
1 cup of dry breadcrumbs
olive oil

Serves: 4
Preparation time: 50 minutes
Cooking time: 10 minutes

Place the fresh breadcrumbs in a bowl with the milk and soak for 30 minutes. Squeeze out any excess milk and combine the breadcrumbs with the meat, cheese, eggs and parsley. Season to taste with salt and pepper. Use your hands to combine into a smooth, uniform mixture, then form it into small meatballs and roll them in the dried breadcrumbs. Heat the oil in a heavy-bottomed pan and gently fry the meatballs until golden brown all over. Remove to paper towels and serve hot.

Marco " My kids love this dish although the adults seem to like it just as much. Buy the best meat you can afford, such as rump or sirloin, as they are full of flavour. The kids enjoy their meatballs with a simple tomato sauce and fusilli pasta or with Cannellini della Nonna (see page 178) and mashed potatoes. Anything that keeps my children well fed, happy and above all QUIET is great with me! "

POLLO AI PEPERONI

Chicken with peppers

3 tablespoons extra virgin olive oil

50 g butter, plus a little extra to
serve

1 organic chicken (approx 2.5 kg),
cut into 8 pieces plus its liver (or
150 g chicken livers if bought
separately)

2 red peppers, de-seeded and finely
sliced

2 yellow peppers, de-seeded and
finely sliced

2 medium onions, finely chopped

1 garlic clove, finely chopped

2 tablespoons tomato purée,
dissolved in 30 ml hot water

5 sage leaves

sea salt and freshly ground black
pepper

50 g pancetta, finely chopped

175 ml white wine

5 basil leaves

Serves: 4
Preparation time: 10 minutes
Cooking time: 1½ hours

In a large saucepan, warm the olive oil and half the butter, add the chicken pieces and brown thoroughly.

Add the peppers, onions, garlic, dissolved tomato purée and sage leaves to the pan. Season with salt and pepper, and gently simmer on a low heat while you cook the livers.

In a separate pan, melt the remaining butter, add the pancetta and livers and fry over a fairly high heat for a few minutes, until the livers start to colour and shrink slightly.

Empty the livers and pancetta into the chicken and peppers, cover with a lid and simmer over a low heat for 1 hour.

Add the wine, bring to the boil for a few minutes to evaporate the alcohol, then reduce the heat, cover and cook for a further 20 minutes.

To serve, top with the fresh basil leaves and a large knob of butter.

Marco "This is the kind of food my mother would have cooked. In her day it was still possible to buy slightly older birds that were a bit tougher and required cooking a little longer but had a wonderful, slightly gamey flavour. Today older birds are very hard to find so I buy the best chicken I can find and cook it on a slightly lower heat for longer. I love this with some good old fashioned mashed potato. "

111

BISTECCA ALLA PIZZAIOLA

Steak with garlic, oregano and tomatoes

4 tablespoons extra virgin olive oil
2 garlic cloves, very thinly sliced
800 g rump beef steak, finely sliced
  (get your butcher to slice the
  steak and you can beat the slices
  with a meat mallet until
  approximately 1 cm thick)
salt and freshly ground black
  pepper
2 x 400 g tins of Italian tomatoes,
  sieved
a large handful of fresh flat leaf
  parsley
2 tablespoons chopped fresh
  oregano or 1 teaspoon dried
  oregano
a small wine glass of white wine

Serves: 4
Preparation time: 15 minutes
Cooking time: 35 minutes

Gently warm the olive oil in a frying pan large enough to hold the beef slices (or cook in 2 batches). Add the garlic and fry over a medium to low heat, until the garlic begins to turn golden. Season the beef slices with salt and pepper, add to the frying pan and cook for about a minute on each side, until the slices are cooked through but still tender.

Remove the steak from the pan and set aside. In the same frying pan, add the tomatoes, most of the parsley, oregano and wine, bring to the boil, then reduce the heat, cover with a lid and cook gently for about 15 minutes or until the sauce has thickened. Return the meat to the pan, season to taste and then simmer gently for a couple of minutes to heat the steak through. To serve, sprinkle with the remaining parsley.

Marco **"** This dish hails from the pizza makers of Naples who would cook this in their wood-fired ovens using the ingredients they had to hand: namely, tomatoes, garlic and oregano. Their trick was to use a razor blade to shave the garlic very finely so that it would dissolve in the sauce. I like to serve this with some salad leaves and some bread on the side to mop up the sauce. **"**

ARISTA DI MAIALE AL FINOCCHIO

Roast pork with fennel

1 sprig of rosemary
4 garlic cloves
sea salt and freshly ground pepper
2½ teaspoons fennel seeds
1.2 kg pork loin, bones split
50 g butter
1 tablespoon extra virgin olive oil
1 fennel bulb
125 ml milk
225 ml dry white wine

Serves: 4
Preparation time: 20 minutes
Cooking time: 2¼ hours

Preheat the oven to 170°C/325°C/Gas Mark 3.

Finely chop the rosemary and garlic. Add the salt, pepper and fennel seeds. Stuff this mixture into the cuts in the pork where the bones were split. Put the meat in a roasting pan with 25 g of the butter and the olive oil, place in the oven and cook for 2 hours.

Roughly chop the fennel, then place in a covered saucepan and cook over a low heat with a little water and the remaining butter until tender. Place in a blender with the milk and blend until perfectly smooth.

When the meat is cooked, cut into slices about ¼ cm thick and arrange on a large serving platter. Keep warm. Pour off the fat from the roasting pan and deglaze with the white wine. Boil for a couple of minutes then strain, add to the fennel and milk mixture and pour over the meat. Additional fennel sauce may be served separately at the table.

Frankie " The Italians love their pork and each region in Italy has its own special way to season and flavour the loin for roasting. This is one of my favourites as the fennel, garlic and rosemary really complement the pork. I love it served with crunchy roast potatoes, lots of veggies and, while apple sauce is not exactly 'la cucina italiana', I think it goes brilliantly with pork. "

AGNELLO AL FORNO

Oven-cooked lamb

2.5 kg cubed lamb meat, largish
  chunks (shoulder meat has more
  flavour and is perfect for this
  dish)
3 medium onions
1 kg potatoes, peeled and cut into
  chunks
3 garlic cloves, crushed
200 ml vegetable stock
1 small wine glass of white wine
small handful of chopped flat leaf
  parsley
small handful of chopped fresh basil
2 tablespoons fresh oregano
  (or 2 teaspoons dried)
sea salt and freshly ground black
  pepper
1 kg ripe tomatoes, roughly
  chopped
2 tablespoons unsalted butter
4 tablespoons extra virgin olive oil
a pinch of sugar

Serves: 4
Preparation time: 15 minutes
Cooking time: 2¼–3¼ hours

Preheat the oven to 180°C/350°F/Gas Mark 4.

Butter a large casserole dish. Wipe the lamb chunks with paper towels and place in the dish; add the onions, potatoes, garlic, stock and wine. Sprinkle over the parsley, basil and oregano and season well with salt and pepper. Top with the chopped tomatoes, sprinkle with the sugar, dot with butter and drizzle with olive oil. Bake, covered, for 2–3 hours, then uncover, check the seasoning and cook uncovered for a further 15 minutes.

Frankie " This dish from Naples derives from 'la cucina povera' (poor man's cuisine). My grandmother would cook this if someone needed feeding up due to illness or 'lo stress'. She would leave it in her wood-fired oven overnight so the meat cooked very slowly and would melt in the mouth. "

115

PESCE

FISH

CACCIUCCO
Fish soup

SPIEDINI ALLA MARINARA
Grilled seafood skewers

SARDINE CON SALMORIGLIO
Grilled sardines with salmoriglio

TRANCIO DI ROMBO ARROSTO
CON OLIVE E POMODORINI
Roasted brill with olives
and baby tomatoes

SCALLOPPINE DI SALMONE
ALLA NAPOLETANA
Salmon fillets in a tomato and garlic sauce

TONNO ALLA MEDITERRANEA
Grilled Mediterranean tuna

PESCE SPADA STEMPERATO
Swordfish stemperato

CODA DI ROSPO AL LIMONE
Monkfish with lemon

BACCALÀ CON OLIVE
Dried salt cod with olives

CALAMARI RIPIENI ALLA GRIGLIA
Grilled stuffed squid

TROTA ALLA MONTANARA
Trout in white wine and chilli

CACCIUCCO

Fish soup

FOR THE FISH STOCK

50 g butter
2 tablespoons olive oil
prawn heads and shells
   (see soup ingredients)
1 large glass dry
   white wine
300 ml water
sea salt

Serves: 4–6
Preparation time:
30 minutes
Cooking time: 1¼ hours

FOR THE SOUP

3 tablespoons olive oil
1 medium onion, finely
   chopped
1 stalk celery, finely
   chopped
2 garlic cloves, finely
   chopped
400 g tin tinned tomatoes
a handful chopped
   fresh parsley
1 tablespoon chopped
   fresh rosemary
1 teaspoon dried red chilli
1 large wine glass dry
   white wine
200 ml water
500 g firm white fish
   such as cod, monkfish,
   roughly filleted and cut
   into 5 cm pieces
500 g sea bass fillet, cut
   into 5 cm pieces
500 g uncooked large
   prawns, peeled, shelled
   and de-headed
300 g cleaned squid,
   bodies cut into 1 cm
   wide rings, tentacles left
   whole
extra chopped fresh parsley
sea salt
extra virgin olive oil

First make your fish stock. Heat the butter and olive oil in a saucepan. Add the prawn heads and shells, bring to a high sizzle, then add the wine. Boil rapidly until the wine has evaporated, Then add the water and simmer gently for 15 minutes. Season to taste with sea salt, strain twice through a fine sieve and set aside.

Heat the oil in a large pot over a medium heat. Add the onion, celery and garlic, cook on a lively simmer for 10 minutes then add the tomatoes, parsley, rosemary and chilli and simmer for a further 2 minutes. Add the wine and cook until the liquid evaporates before adding the stock. Bring to the boil, reduce the heat and simmer gently for 20 minutes.

Add all the seafood to the soup base. Cook until just opaque, for about 4 minutes. Adjust seasoning to taste then ladle the soup and fish into 4 bowls. Sprinkle with additional parsley and sea salt and drizzle with olive oil.

Marco   " This seafood soup, called Cacciucco (meaning 'concoction'), is a speciality of Livorno, a fishing port and Tuscany's second-largest city. The recipe stems from the late 18th century and variations of it appear all along the Tuscan coast. Traditionally, at least five types of fish and shellfish are included (one for each 'c' in the name), and it is best to use whatever is in season. If you like it spicy, just add more chilli. "

SPIEDINI ALLA MARINARA

Grilled seafood skewers

2 kg assorted seafood. Choose at least 3 from any of the following: squid, large prawns, monkfish (or any firm white fish), sea bream, cooked octopus, scallops, eel and, if you possibly can, lobster tails. Ask your fishmonger to de-scale, gut and fillet the whole fish.

5 tablespoons extra virgin olive oil

2 garlic cloves, crushed

2 tablespoons chopped fresh flat leaf parsley

2 lemons, cut into wedges, to garnish

Serves: 4
Preparation time: 15 minutes
Cooking time: 5 minutes

Prepare the charcoal fire, barbecue or grill, until hot.

Carefully wash all the seafood. If using squid, remove the inner bone (which is similar to a piece of plastic). If using lobster tails, take out the meat in one piece, and de-head the prawns if you have bought these. Then carefully slice all the fish and seafood (except the prawns) into 5 cm pieces.

In a small pan, warm the olive oil, add the garlic and fry until golden. Remove from the heat and then add the parsley.

Thread alternate pieces of the seafood and fish on to the skewers. Then brush on the garlicky olive oil mixture (using a pastry brush, and reserving a little oil for serving) and place on the hot barbecue or grill, close to the heat.

Cook the skewers quickly for 1–2 minutes on each side, or until they are cooked through (but don't overcook, as the fish will toughen and lose its flavour).

To serve, place the skewers on a large platter, drizzle with the remaining olive oil and garnish with lemon wedges. *Buon appetito!*

Frankie " Spiedini are enormously popular all over Italy and they are one of my favourite barbecue dishes as they're delicious but really healthy. The fish must be spanking fresh and the coals very, very hot. I love going to the fish market with my mother in Sardinia – she chooses the fish, I carry the bags. Some things never change ... "

SARDINE CON SALMORIGLIO

Grilled sardines with salmoriglio

1 large red Treviso or raddichio
 lettuce
3 tablespoons extra virgin olive oil
3 teaspoons white wine vinegar
16 large sardines, cleaned, heads
 and tails cut off
salt

FOR THE SALMORIGLIO:

zest of 2 lemons, cut into strips and
 brought to the boil 3 times in cold
 water, refreshing after each time
40 g capers, drained and washed
1 handful of black olives, stoned
 and halved
1 large handful of fresh flat leaf
 parsley, stalks removed and
 finely chopped

Serves: 4
Preparation time: 40 minutes
Cooking time: 7 minutes

Prepare the salmoriglio by mixing together all the ingredients and putting to one side.

Quarter the lettuce and lightly fry in a pan with a little olive oil for 2 minutes until very lightly browned but still crisp. Add the vinegar, cover with tin foil and set aside in a warm place. Brush the sardines with olive oil, season with salt and cook under a hot grill for approximately 2½ minutes on each side, until the skin is crispy and slightly charred. To serve, divide the sardines between 4 plates and place the lettuce on one side of the fish. Sprinkle the salmoriglio over the top of the sardines. Drizzle with olive oil and season with salt.

Frankie " This dish is very simple but reminiscent of so many superb holidays spent by the sea in Italy. Salmoriglio is a dry sauce used mainly to accompany fish. It's a magnificent addition to smoky, grilled sardines and complements their slightly oily texture perfectly. Whenever I have this, and wherever I am, I swear I can feel the sand between my toes and the sun on my face. *Che bello far' niente.* "

TRANCIO DI ROMBO ARROSTO CON OLIVE E POMODORINI

Roasted brill with olives and baby tomatoes

5 tablespoons extra virgin olive oil
1 whole garlic clove
15 large green olives, flesh cut off the stones in 2 discs, 1 from each side
20 or so whole cherry tomatoes, washed
1 wine glass of very dry white wine
100 ml fish or vegetable stock
4 x 250 g brill steaks on the bone
sea salt and freshly ground white pepper
2 tablespoons chopped parsley

Serves: 4
Preparation time: 20 minutes
Cooking time: 15 minutes

Heat 2 tablespoons of olive oil in a saucepan and add the whole clove of garlic, the olives and the tomatoes and cook gently for 3 minutes without colouring. Turn up the heat and add the wine, boil until all the wine has evaporated, then add the stock, bring back to a gentle simmer and allow to cook gently for a further 3 minutes, taking care not to break the tomatoes. Turn off the heat, remove the garlic clove and keep warm.

Add 3 tablespoons of olive oil to a non-stick frying pan. Season the brill steaks and fry them skin-side down. When you can see that the skin is turning golden and crunchy and the flesh is going from translucent to white almost to the top, turn the steaks over then turn the heat off and allow them to rest in the pan. Keep warm.

To serve, reheat the olive and tomato sauce, stir in the parsley and place 2 spoonfuls in the centre of 4 warmed plates, top with brill and then with the juices from the pan.

Frankie " This is a wonderful combination of sea and earth. The delicate flavour of the fish is complemented beautifully by the earthy flavours of the olives and tomatoes. "

SCALLOPPINE DI SALMONE ALLA NAPOLETANA

Salmon fillets in a tomato and garlic sauce

100 g cherry tomatoes, halved
20 black olives, stoned and halved
6 tablespoons extra virgin olive oil
4 fillets of wild Scottish salmon
   (approximately 200 g each)
4 anchovy fillets, chopped
a small handful of fresh basil leaves
sea salt

Serves: 4
Preparation time: 10 minutes
Cooking time: 5 minutes

Place the cherry tomatoes, olives and olive oil in a pan on a low heat until just warmed. Put the salmon in a hot, non-stick frying pan and cook for about 1 minute on each side (it should remain pink in the middle). To serve, place each salmon piece on a plate, spoon a quarter of the tomato garnish and an anchovy over the top, add 4 or 5 basil leaves and sprinkle with sea salt.

Frankie " Naples, the city that gives its name to this dish, has a cuisine of which the 'Napoletani' are justifiably proud. The big, robust flavours of the holy trinity of Neapolitan cooking – anchovies, black olives and tomatoes – lend themselves brilliantly to an assortment of meat, fish and vegetable dishes. "

TONNO ALLA MEDITERRANEO

Grilled Mediterranean tuna

150 g cherry tomatoes, halved

20 g black olives, stoned and halved

20 g fine capers, drained and washed

100 ml extra virgin olive oil, plus a little extra for grilling

4 tuna steaks (approximately 200 g each)

a small handful of fresh basil leaves

sea salt

Serves: 4
Preparation time: 10 minutes
Cooking time: 5 minutes

Place the cherry tomatoes, olives, capers and olive oil in a pan and warm over a low heat until tepid. Preheat a grill pan that has been brushed with olive oil, add the tuna steaks and grill under a high heat for approximately 1 minute on each side, until the tuna is cooked but pink in the middle.

To serve, place the tuna steaks on 4 plates, spoon over the tomato garnish and top with the basil leaves and a sprinkling of sea salt.

Frankie ❝ I cook this dish at home when Catherine and I have an evening to ourselves and can relax. It takes very little time to prepare and needs no other vegetables other than a bit of salad. Because it's so easy to make, it's light on the washing up which keeps my wife happy, and if she's happy ... I'm happy. ❞

PESCE SPADA STEMPERATO

Swordfish stemperato

500 g waxy potatoes
6 tablespoons of
    extra virgin olive oil
2 large onions, finely chopped
12 green olives, stoned and
    chopped
4 plum tomatoes, chopped
1 teaspoon dried chilli flakes
2 tablespoons capers, drained and
    washed
4 teaspoons sugar
4 tablespoons red wine vinegar
sea salt and freshly ground black
    pepper
4 medium swordfish steaks
plain flour
a handful of chopped fresh flat leaf
    parsley

Serves: 4
Preparation time: 30 minutes
Cooking time: 25 minutes

Preheat the oven to180°C/350°F/Gas Mark 4. Peel the potatoes and boil for 20 minutes, until tender. Allow to cool and cut into 1 cm thick slices.

Over a medium heat, fry the onions in 2 tablespoons of olive oil, until softened. Add the olives, cook for a few minutes more, and then add the tomatoes. Simmer for 5 minutes, stirring occasionally. Then add the chilli flakes, capers, sugar and red wine vinegar, and cook over a high heat for a couple of minutes to evaporate the vinegar. Season to taste and set aside.

Cover the swordfish steaks with seasoned flour. Heat 4 tablespoons of olive oil in a pan and fry the steaks over a medium heat for 2 minutes on each side. Lightly grease a glass baking dish, big enough to hold all the ingredients, cover the base with slices of potato, then layer with the swordfish steaks and cover with the tomato sauce. Bake for 10 minutes, sprinkle with the chopped parsley, and serve.

Frankie " The word 'stemperato' refers to the typically Sicilian process by which the vinegar evaporates during cooking. A good and very old friend of mine is 'siciliano' and this is something his mother used to cook for us quite often. It's all about big earthy flavours: the sweet and sour of the vinegar and the sugar, the capers, the chilli and the olives all blending together. It's a one-pot dish that is perfect for supper with friends as you can prepare it during the day and shove it in the oven just before you eat. "

135

CODA DI ROSPO AL LIMONE

Monkfish with lemon

1 kg monkfish tail, ask your
    fishmonger to remove the
    membrane
2 garlic cloves, very thinly sliced
sea salt
2 lemons
½ teaspoon sugar
150 ml extra virgin olive oil

Serves: 4
Preparation time: 10 minutes
Cooking time: 40 minutes

Preheat the oven to 200°C/400°F/Gas Mark 6.

Make a few slits in the flesh of the monkfish (especially around the bone area) and insert the garlic slivers. Season with salt and place in an oven-proof dish. Squeeze the juice from 1 of the lemons and whisk with the sugar and half the olive oil until it's the consistency of thin cream. Pour over the fish.

Remove the zest from the remaining lemon and slice it into thin strips, removing all traces of the pith. Sprinkle the lemon strips over the fish and cook in the oven for 40 minutes. Once cooked, drain off the liquid, strain it through a sieve and whisk in the remaining olive oil. To serve, place the fish on a heated plate, and pour the sauce around the outside of the dish.

Frankie " This is a very simple dish from Sicily where the lemons are as sweet as oranges and can be eaten in the same way. To compensate for the lack of sweetness found in most other lemons, I add a little sugar to the marinade. This is a great dish for a light Sunday lunch, with a glass of sparkling Prosecco and a few mixed leaves to mop up the juices from the fish. "

BACCALÀ CON OLIVE

Dried salt cod with olives

450 g dried salt cod
125 ml extra virgin olive oil
1 onion, finely chopped
2 garlic cloves, finely chopped
1 carrot, finely chopped
1 celery stick, finely chopped
450 g ripe tomatoes, peeled and
    roughly chopped
750 g King Edward or similar
    floury potatoes, peeled and
    cubed
100 ml hot water
100 g green olives, stoned and
    roughly chopped
50 g pine nuts, toasted
1 large wine glass of white wine
sea salt and freshly ground black
    pepper

Serves: 4
Preparation time: 20 minutes
Cooking time: 30 minutes
Soaking time: 48 hours

Soak the cod in cold water for two days, changing the water approximately every 8 hours. Then drain and dry it, and cut it into bite-size pieces.

Heat the olive oil in a large pan, add the onion, garlic, carrot and celery and fry over a moderate heat, until the vegetables start to brown. Add the cod pieces, tomatoes, potatoes and water, and cook for 20 minutes, stirring gently once or twice. Add the olives, pine nuts and wine, increase the heat, and boil for a few minutes to allow the alcohol to evaporate. Season to taste, arrange on a warmed platter and serve.

Frankie " Salt cod doesn't sound particularly appetizing but, trust me, it's so good that you'll want to make it again and again. You can buy salt cod in most Italian or Spanish delis and it's reasonably inexpensive. In Italy, it's traditionally eaten on Christmas Eve and, as ever, each region has its own version. This is the Sicilian version and it's almost like a fish stew. "

CALAMARI RIPIENI ALLA GRIGLIA

Grilled stuffed squid

4 whole squid, cleaned, body sacs
  and tentacles separated by your
  fishmonger
1 small fresh red chilli, de-seeded
  and finely chopped
1 small garlic clove, finely chopped
a handful of chopped fresh flat leaf
  parsley
50 g fresh breadcrumbs
1 tablespoon tomato purée
juice of ½ lemon plus 2 lemons cut
  in half, to serve
extra virgin olive oil
sea salt and freshly ground black
  pepper
4 cocktail sticks

Serves: 4
Preparation time: 25 minutes
Cooking time: 5 minutes

Preheat the grill to a medium temperature.

Chop the squid tentacles, place them in a bowl and mix in the chilli, garlic, parsley, breadcrumbs, tomato purée and lemon juice. Then drizzle in 2 tablespoons of the olive oil and mix well.

Spoon the mixture into the squids' body sacs and secure with cocktail sticks so that the stuffing does not seep out during cooking.

Brush each of the squid with a little olive oil and place in the grill for a few minutes, turning frequently, until golden brown and tender.

Serve with the lemon halves.

Frankie " I love calamari when it's been cooked on the barbecue but, let's face it, in England the weather's not always on your side. So I've adapted this so you can grill it indoors and it will taste just as good – well almost. The idea is not to buy the squid too large as the bigger they are, the tougher they taste. "

TROTA ALLA MONTANARA

Trout in white wine and chilli

6 tablespoons extra virgin olive oil
3 garlic cloves, finely chopped
1 small fresh red chilli, de-seeded
    and finely chopped
a small handful of fresh flat leaf
    parsley, finely chopped
3 tablespoons tomato purée,
    dissolved in 4 tablespoons hot
    water
2 wine glasses of dry white wine
6 basil leaves, roughly chopped
100 g unsalted butter
sea salt and freshly ground black
    pepper
plain flour
4 medium trout, gutted and cleaned
a pinch of sugar

Serves: 4
Preparation time: 20 minutes
Cooking time: 10 minutes

Heat the olive oil in a saucepan, then add the garlic, chilli and parsley and gently fry for a few minutes, until softened. Add the dissolved tomato purée, wine and basil leaves, increase the heat and cook for a few minutes to boil off the alcohol. Remove from the heat and allow it to infuse while you prepare the fish.

Heat the butter in a large frying pan (reserving a knob to mix in later). Season and lightly flour the trout, add them to the frying pan and sauté over a low heat for a couple of minutes, until golden on both sides but not quite cooked. Meanwhile, put the sauce back on to the heat, bring it back to a gentle simmer and whisk in the sugar and remaining knob of butter. Then pour the sauce into the frying pan with the trout and simmer gently for a few minutes, until the trout is fully cooked. Serve immediately, spooning the sauce over each portion.

Marco " This is a recipe that reminds me of childhood days spent fishing. Although trout has a very delicate flavour and lends itself to being simply grilled with a little lemon, Italians also like to give it a real boost with gutsy flavours. I love chilli so tend to be a little overgenerous when cooking with it, so perhaps half a chilli would be better for the faint of heart. "

PIZZA E PANE

PIZZA AND BREAD

PIZZA POMODORO
Basic pizza base
with tomato topping

MARGHERITA
Tomato and Mozzarella

BASILICO
Tomato, Mozzarella and basil

AMERICANA
Tomato, Mozzarella and pepperoni

FRANKIE'S PIZZA
Tomato, Mozzarella,
Parma ham and rocket

NAPOLETANA
Tomato, Mozzarella, anchovies,
black olives and capers

FUNGHI PORCINI
Tomato, Mozzarella and
porcini mushrooms

PANE
Bread

PANE ALL'AGLIO E ROSMARINO
Garlic bread with rosemary

PIZZA POMODORO

Basic pizza base with tomato topping

FOR THE DOUGH:

10 g yeast
300 ml water
10 ml olive oil
450 g Tipo 00 flour
pinch of salt

FOR THE TOMATO TOPPING:

4 tinned plum tomatoes
1 basil leaf
130 ml olive oil
30 g salt

Makes: enough for 4 pizza bases
Preparation time: 50 minutes

Dissolve the yeast in tepid water and add the olive oil.

Mix together the flour and salt and pour in the yeast liquid. Combine until it forms a smooth dough.

Divide the dough into 4 equal balls then cover with a damp cloth. Leave to rise for 30 minutes.

Put the tray you intend to cook your pizza on into the oven and preheat it to 240°C/475°F/Gas Mark 9.

Dust the dough balls with flour and use your fingers to tease them out into pizza base shapes, approximately 25 cm wide and ½ cm thick.

For the tomato topping, simply blitz together the ingredients in a food processor. Then add any of the pizza toppings from the following recipes.

Frankie 66 Pizza is definitely an Italian dish and therefore should be cooked the Italian way. This means losing the thick base, pineapple, curried chicken and any hint of cheddar cheese! A real pizza should be wafer thin with a golden bottom and topped with two, or maybe even three, carefully chosen ingredients rather than the entire kitchen sink variety that we've become accustomed to ordering. 99

MARGHERITA

Tomato and Mozzarella

2 tablespoons tomato topping
  (page 148)
½ ball of buffalo Mozzarella, grated
8 basil leaves, roughly torn

Makes: enough for 1 pizza
Preparation time: 3 minutes
Cooking time: 10 minutes

Spread the tomato topping onto the prepared pizza base.

Sprinkle the Mozzarella over the pizza then bake in the oven on the pre-heated tray for 10 minutes.

Scatter the basil leaves over the pizza then serve immediately.

BASILICO

Tomato, Mozzarella and basil

2 tablespoons tomato topping
    (page 148)
½ ball of buffalo Mozzarella,
    grated or cubed
6 cherry tomatoes, quartered
8 basil leaves, roughly torn
drizzle of olive oil

Makes: enough for one pizza
Preparation time: 5 minutes
Cooking time: 10 minutes

Spread the tomato topping onto the prepared pizza base then bake in the oven on the preheated tray for 10 minutes.

Remove from the oven then sprinkle over the Mozzarella, cherry tomatoes and basil leaves. Drizzle with olive oil and serve immediately.

AMERICANA

Tomato, Mozzarella and pepperoni

2 tablespoons tomato topping
   (page 148)
½ ball of buffalo Mozzarella,
   grated or cubed
30 g sliced pepperoni

Makes: enough for 1 pizza
Preparation time: 3 minutes
Cooking time: 10 minutes

Spread the tomato topping onto the prepared pizza base.

Sprinkle the Mozzarella over the pizza then scatter the pepperoni slices on top. Bake in the oven on the preheated tray for 10 minutes.

Remove from the oven and serve immediately.

FRANKIE'S PIZZA

Tomato, Mozzarella, Parma ham and rocket

2 tablespoons tomato topping
    (page 148)
½ ball of buffalo Mozzarella,
    grated or cubed
1 beef tomato, sliced
4 slices of Parma ham
small handful of rocket leaves
15 g Parmesan
drizzle of olive oil

Makes: enough for 1 pizza
Preparation time: 5 minutes
Cooking time: 10 minutes

Spread the tomato topping onto the prepared pizza base.

Sprinkle the Mozzarella over the pizza then bake in the oven on the pre-heated tray for 10 minutes.

Remove the base from the oven then arrange the tomato, Parma ham and rocket leaves on top. Scatter over the Parmesan and drizzle with the olive oil. Serve immediately.

NAPOLETANA

Tomato, Mozzarella, anchovies, black olives and capers

2 tablespoons tomato topping
(page 148)
½ ball of buffalo Mozzarella,
grated or cubed
6 olives
1 teaspoon capers
5 anchovies

Makes: enough for 1 pizza
Preparation time: 3 minutes
Cooking time: 10 minutes

Spread the tomato topping onto the prepared pizza base.

Sprinkle the mozzarella over the pizza then arrange the olives, capers and anchovies on top.

Bake in the oven on the preheated tray for 10 minutes then serve immediately.

FUNGHI PORCINI

Tomato, Mozzarella and porcini mushrooms

2 tablespoons tomato topping
    (page 148)
½ ball of buffalo Mozzarella,
    grated or cubed
3–4 fresh porcini mushrooms,
    sliced
4 cherry tomatoes, halved

Makes: enough for 1 pizza
Preparation time: 3 minutes
Cooking time: 10 minutes

Spread the tomato topping onto the prepared pizza base.

Sprinkle the Mozzarella over the pizza then arrange the mushrooms and tomatoes on top.

Bake in the oven on the preheated tray for 10 minutes then serve immediately.

PANE

Bread

1 kg strong white bread flour
1 tablespoon sea salt
650 ml lukewarm water
15 g dried yeast
1 tablespoon Demerara sugar

Makes: 2 loaves
Preparation time: 1 hour
Cooking time: 30 minutes

Pre-heat the oven to 210°C/410°F/Gas Mark 5. Pile the flour onto a clean, dry work surface and sprinkle with the salt, then make a well in the centre. Pour half the water into the well, then add the yeast and sugar. Stir the flour in the centre of the well into the water with a fork until you have a porridge consistency in the middle of the flour. Wait until the yeast starts to froth, then add the rest of the water and combine well with the remaining flour until you have a dough. Knead for at least 10 minutes (whispering sweet nothings as you go) by rolling the dough backwards and forwards twice then using one hand to pull it towards you and the other hand to push it away. Repeat this kneading process until you have a totally smooth dough.

Place the dough in a bowl, cover with Clingfilm and leave it in a warm place to rise for half an hour until it has doubled in size (this may take slightly longer if your kitchen isn't very warm). Next knock the air out of the dough by thumping it on the work surface and kneading it for about 30 seconds.

Split the dough in half, shape to your specification, and place in your loaf tins or on a baking tray. Leave it to prove for a further 20 minutes (again somewhere warm).

Make two diagonal slashes in the top of each loaf and bake for 30 minutes or so, depending on the size of your tin. The best way to tell when bread is ready is by tapping the bottom of the loaf, if it sounds hollow it's done, if not return it to the oven for a little longer before checking again. Allow the bread to cool before attempting to cut it.

Frankie " A lot, and I mean a helluva lot, of bread is eaten in Italy. It is the first thing to hit the table, be it breakfast, lunch or dinner and it is eaten freely throughout every course. It would be unthinkable for an Italian to eat without bread. There is a wonderful Italian phrase which we use to talk about someone really boring: 'E peggio di una giornata senza pane'. Literally translated it means, 'Being with him/her is worse than a having to go a whole day without bread', which for most Italians is nearly impossible! This is a recipe for basic bread dough from my grandmother who swore that the bread rose higher and tasted better if she talked to it as she made it. "

PANE ALL'AGLIO E ROSMARINO

Garlic bread with rosemary

1 batch of basic dough
   (see p. 162)
2 cloves garlic, peeled
a handful of fresh rosemary needles
salt crystals
4 anchovy fillets, soaked in milk to
   remove the salt
3 tablespoons of olive oil
black pepper

Makes: approx 12 rolls
Preparation time: 1 hour 10 minutes
Cooking time: 20–25 minutes

Preheat the oven to 200°C/392°F/Gas Mark 4. Follow the basic bread dough instructions on p.160 up to the point where you have knocked the air out of the dough.

Crush the cloves of garlic and the rosemary needles with a few salt crystals in a pestle and mortar. Add the anchovy fillets, pound a little more then stir in the olive oil. Add a few pinches of black pepper.

Place the dough on a clean work surface and flatten it out roughly with the palm of your hand. Sprinkle with the garlic and rosemary mixture, fold the dough over then knead well. Tear off small bits of the dough and shape into rolls. Place on a baking tray and leave to rise for 30 minutes.

Bake in the oven for 20–25 minutes until golden brown.

Frankie " This smells divine as it cooks. It's a world away from the regular garlic bread that we know today, which is actually quite horrid and tends to come out of the freezer compartment of most supermarkets. If you can, always try to make your own. When you eat it with a big old mixed salad dressed with a good balsamic vinegar and some spicy extra virgin olive oil it's a meal in itself. You can pretty much add anything you want to this. Try adding a few shreds of ripped up Parma ham when it's cooked or even a little Italian sausage crumbled over the top when it's baking. Be adventurous ... experiment a little "

CONTORNI

SIDE DISHES

ASPARAGI AL PARMIGIANO
Asparagus with Parmesan

PISELLI ALLA FRANCESE
French-style peas

PARMIGIANA DI MELANZANE
Aubergine Parmigiana

CANNELLINI DELLA NONNA
Nonna's cannellini beans

FUNGHI TRIFOLATI
Sautéed mushrooms with garlic

ZUCCHINI RIPIENI
Stuffed courgette

BROCCOLI AL VINO ROSSO
Broccoli braised in red wine

FRITTATA

CIPOLLINE CON PANCETTA
Baby onions with pancetta

FAGIOLINI AL POMODORO
French beans with tomato and basil

TORTA DI PATATE
Potato cake

BAGNA CAUDA
Anchovy, chilli and garlic dip

ASPARAGI AL PARMIGIANO

Asparagus with Parmesan

24 medium asparagus spears
12 sage leaves
40 g finely grated Parmesan
100 g unsalted butter

Serves: 4
Preparation time: 5 minutes
Cooking time: 8 minutes

Blanch the asparagus spears in boiling, salted water for 3 minutes, then dunk in a bowl of ice cold water. This ensures the asparagus keeps its colour and halts the cooking process.

Divide the asparagus between 4 plates, layer on 3 sage leaves per plate, and then sprinkle with the Parmesan cheese. Top with the butter, divided equally between the 4 servings. Heat under a hot grill until the butter and cheese have melted.

Serve immediately.

Frankie " I can't argue that classic asparagus hollandaise isn't very good, but I prefer my asparagus served more simply to let its delicate flavour shine through. This recipe is a perfect way to do just that. The sage 'lifts' the dish and is fabulous with Parmigiano. "

PISELLI ALLA FRANCESE

French-style peas

2 tablespoons unsalted butter
1 small onion, very finely chopped
1 small carrot, very finely sliced
   then diced
½ kg fresh peas, shelled
150 g very good ham, preferably
   sliced off the bone, cut into strips

Serves: 4
Preparation time: 10 minutes
Cooking time: 30 minutes

Heat the butter and add the onion and carrot, cooking gently over a low heat for about 5 minutes. Allow to soften without browning.

Add the peas and a couple of tablespoons of water and simmer very gently for 5 minutes.

Add the ham and a little more water if necessary. Continue to simmer gently for 20–30 minutes until the peas are tender, adding tiny amounts of water if required.

Frankie " This Roman dish was my favourite supper for years and years whilst I was growing up and I can always remember eating it with dad who loved it just as much. Mum would make it a lot, at least twice a week, and it's the first thing I want to eat when I visit my mother at home in Milan – no one makes it quite like her. The little bit of ham gives extra texture and flavour. "

175

PARMIGIANA DI MELANZANE

Aubergine Parmigiana

1 kg aubergines
extra virgin olive oil
Sea salt and freshly ground black
  pepper
2 garlic cloves, chopped
3 x 400 g good quality tinned
  tomatoes, sieved and chopped
a small handful of fresh basil leaves
a large handful of finely grated
  Parmesan
1½ kg fresh Mozzarella, cubed

Serves: 8
Preparation time: 3 hours
Cooking time: 50 minutes

Preheat the oven to 180°C/350°F/Gas Mark 4.

Cut the aubergines in ½cm strips, lengthways. Sprinkle each slice with salt and layer on a plate. Cover with a plate of the same size and add a heavy weight on top (such as a large bottle of water) so that water can be squeezed out of the aubergines. Set aside for 2–3 hours.

Meanwhile, heat 2 tablespoons of olive oil in a saucepan, add the garlic and fry until slightly golden. Add the tomatoes and basil and cook over a medium heat for 25 minutes, until the sauce thickens. Season to taste.

Remove the weight from the aubergine, thoroughly rinse the slices and pat dry. Generously cover the bottom of a large frying pan with olive oil and place over a high heat. In batches, brown the aubergine slices on both sides, lowering the heat and adding oil as required. Drain the slices on kitchen roll as you go along.

Cover the bottom of a 23 cm × 30 cm ovenproof dish with a thin layer of tomato sauce; add a layer of aubergine slices, then top with a handful of the cheeses. Ladle some tomato sauce over this and continue layering, finishing with one of tomato sauce and a sprinkling of cheeses.

Bake for 15–20 minutes to heat through and melt the Mozzarella then set aside for a few minutes to cool. Cut into squares and serve warm.

Frankie

❝ My father loved this particular dish as, although it's vegetarian, it has the meaty and slightly smoky texture of a good steak. To this day it makes me think of childhood Sunday lunches. ❞

CANNELLINI DELLA NONNA

Nonna's cannellini beans

500 g cannellini beans
1 small onion, whole
1 small carrot, whole
4 garlic cloves, peeled and left
    whole
a sprig of rosemary, a sprig of
    thyme, 4 sage leaves and 4
    sprigs of parsley, all tied with
    string
rind of ½ a lemon, no pith attached,
    kept whole or in large pieces
1 teaspoon sea salt
5 tablespoons extra virgin olive oil
chopped flat leaf parsley, to serve

Serves: 4
Preparation time: 10 minutes
Cooking time: 2½ hours
Soaking time: overnight

Soak the beans in cold water overnight and then drain, refresh and place in a saucepan with the onion, carrot, garlic, bunch of herbs, lemon rind and salt. Cover with cold water and bring to the boil. Cook the beans for about 2 hours until they have softened. Drain and remove the vegetables, garlic cloves and herbs. Take half the beans and purée them into a soft paste then return them to the saucepan with the whole beans. Heat the olive oil gently in a large frying pan and gently warm through the beans. Check the seasoning and serve with freshly chopped parsley.

Frankie " This is such a simple dish from 'la cucina povera' of Italy but is a substantial meal in itself with a bit of bread and cheese with fruit to follow. I enjoy grazing on food rather than eating large portions and when this is in the fridge at home you can be sure I'll be hovering around with a teaspoon for a little 'assaggio' every now and then. It's incredibly healthy and the fresh herbs give the beans that wonderful taste of Italy. "

FUNGHI TRIFOLATI

Sautéed mushrooms with garlic

400 g mixed, preferably wild, fresh
   mushrooms (at least 1 of the
   following: porcini, chanterelles,
   chestnut, oyster)
3 tablespoons extra virgin olive oil
50 g butter
2 garlic cloves, finely chopped
a large handful of fresh flat leaf
   parsley, finely chopped
a small wine glass of white wine

Serves: 4
Preparation time: 15 minutes
Cooking time: 15 minutes

Clean the mushrooms with a damp cloth (do not wash them as they will absorb too much water), then slice them to medium thickness. Warm the olive oil and butter in a large, heavy-based frying pan, add the garlic, the mushrooms and half the parsley and sauté for 8 minutes. Keep the heat quite high but make sure the garlic doesn't burn. Once the mushrooms are soft, turn up the heat and add the white wine. Boil rapidly for a few minutes to allow the alcohol to reduce, then add the rest of the parsley and serve.

Marco 66 This is the classic Italian way of preparing mushrooms, ensuring the flavours shine through. I first went mushrooming as a young boy with my dad and was instantly hooked. We would get up terribly early to trek through the woods. The most prized wild mushrooms are the porcini (boletus edulis). Nothing can beat coming home at 9am with a basket of these precious fungi and cooking Trifolati. 99

179

ZUCCHINI RIPIENI

Stuffed courgette

6 medium courgettes
100 g ricotta cheese
1 egg, separated
50 g chopped flat leaf parsley
60 g grated Parmesan
sea salt and freshly ground pepper
25 g butter

Serves: 4
Preparation time: 25 minutes
Cooking time: 40 minutes

Preheat the oven to 180°C/350°F/Gas Mark 4. Boil the courgettes in salted water for a few minutes, until just tender, then drain and refresh them under cold water.

Cut a 2 cm-wide strip from the middle of each courgette, scraping out and discarding half of the insides.

To make the stuffing, mix the ricotta, egg yolk, parsley and 50 g of the Parmesan, and season to taste. Beat the egg white to stiff peaks and fold it into the stuffing mixture. Using a piping bag (or a small teaspoon if you don't have one), generously fill the courgettes.

Arrange the vegetables in a greased baking dish, dot their tops with butter and bake for 40 minutes, or until the insides are firm and the tops of the courgettes are golden brown. (Keep the courgettes moist by adding a few tablespoons of water to the baking dish, when necessary.) Sprinkle with the remaining Parmesan and serve.

Frankie " The good people of Parma in the Emiglia Romagna region of Italy love to stuff things and vegetables are no exception. This dish is one of my favourites: it's very light but the texture of the courgette together with the intense flavours of the herbs and ricotta and Parmigiano cheeses make it almost like eating pasta. "

BROCCOLI AL VINO ROSSO

Broccoli braised in red wine

500 g broccoli florets
100 g Pecorino cheese, finely
   shaved
1 red onion, finely sliced
10 black olives, stoned and roughly
   chopped
10 anchovy fillets, roughly chopped
½ teaspoon dried red chilli
6 tablespoons extra virgin olive oil
a wine glass of red wine
a small handful of fresh flat leaf
   parsley, finely chopped

Serves: 4
Preparation time: 20 minutes
Cooking time: 15 minutes

Place a layer of broccoli florets in the bottom of a large saucepan. Then add layers of the Pecorino, red onion, olives and anchovies, until all the ingredients are used up.

Add the chilli and drizzle with the olive oil. Cover and simmer very gently over a low heat, until the broccoli is tender. Add the red wine, turn up the heat and simmer for a few minutes to evaporate the alcohol and any excess liquid. Serve with the chopped parsley.

Frankie " This is a very unusual vegetable dish which sounds as though it shouldn't taste nice but in actual fact is gorgeous when served with plain grilled or roasted meat. The sweetness of the onions and the wine meld together to form a really rich sauce that is perfect for dipping bits of steak or chicken in. This dish is one of my discoveries – I found it in an Italian women's magazine ages ago and as it was so unusual I just had to try it. "

FRITTATA

a large knob of butter

2 tablespoons extra virgin olive oil,

2 medium onions, very finely sliced
   (not chopped)

1 courgette, diced

½ red pepper, diced

2 tomatoes, diced

3 cold boiled new potatoes, with
   skins on, diced

7 large organic eggs

salt and freshly ground black
   pepper

a good handful of chopped flat leaf
   parsley

Serves: 4
Preparation time: 20 minutes
Cooking time: 20 minutes

Warm the butter and oil over a fairly high heat and sauté the onions gently until they are soft and a little crisp around the edges. Add all the vegetables, including the potatoes, and allow them to cook until slightly crisp at the edges. Add a little more olive oil if necessary, and take care not to let the vegetable mixture catch and burn in the pan.

Beat the eggs and season well, adding half of the parsley. Turn the heat down to medium and add the eggs, keeping the contents of the pan moving so the egg mixture coats all of the vegetables. Let the frittata cook slowly. As it solidifies, tip the pan so that the liquid egg drains from the top to the bottom, but other than that let it be. When it is quite firm, place a large plate over the frying pan and turn the frittata over onto the plate then slide it, upside down, back into the pan. Let it cook for a further 5 minutes or so on the bottom. To serve, scatter over the remaining parsley. Eat hot or cold.

Marco " This is a dish my mother used to make me when I came home from school for lunch. Frittata is the staple of all Italian picnics and is a great all-round snack if made with care using very fresh organic eggs with the addition of a few simple flavours. This is not a kitchen sink recipe where you can throw everything at it – a little restraint goes a long way. "

CIPOLLINE CON PANCETTA

Baby onions with pancetta

2 tablespoons extra virgin olive oil
150 g pancetta, cubed
500 g baby onions, peeled and left
  whole
5 fresh sage leaves
280 ml water
sea salt

Makes: 500 ml
Preparation time: 10 minutes
Cooking time: 35 minutes

Heat the oil in a saucepan, add the pancetta and fry gently for 5 minutes.

Add the onions and sage leaves and cook over a high heat until the onions are browned all over.

Lower the heat and add the water, season and cook for 30 minutes until the onions are tender but still intact.

Marco " This is a great little standby to have in the fridge as it's perfect served hot or cold. I use it cold as part of an antipasto served with a wedge of cheese and some good bread, or slightly crushed in a meat sandwich of Sunday roast leftovers. Warmed, it's perfect with grilled meat, especially venison or duck, and heating it releases even more of the sweetness from the onions. "

FAGIOLINI AL POMODORO

French beans with tomato and basil

600 g French beans, trimmed
3 tablespoons extra virgin olive oil
1 red onion, finely chopped
2 garlic cloves, finely shaved
200 g tinned tomatoes, sieved to remove the seeds
a pinch of sugar
sea salt and freshly ground black pepper
a large handful of chopped basil leaves

Cook the beans in plenty of boiling, salted water for 10 minutes, until tender. Heat the oil in a frying pan, add the onion and garlic and fry over a low heat until soft (do not allow to brown). Drain the beans and add to the pan, together with the tomatoes and the sugar. Season to taste and simmer gently for 10 minutes, adding a little water if the mixture gets dry. To serve, top with the chopped basil.

Serves: 4
Preparation time: 20 minutes
Cooking time: 25 minutes

Frankie " French beans are very popular in Italy and grown in large quantities in most vegetable patches. There's nothing like a glut of green beans to get the creative juices flowing and Italians have numerous way of making them a little more interesting – this being my favourite. "

TORTA DI PATATE

Potato cake

50 ml extra virgin olive oil

1 kg onions, very finely chopped

200 g sieved tinned tomatoes

3 kg good quality floury potatoes
(King Edwards), cooked in their
skins until tender

100 g butter

100 g grated Pecorino (if you don't
have Pecorino use double the
Parmigiano)

100 g grated Parmigiano

1 large egg yolk

sea salt and freshly ground black
pepper

1 egg, beaten, for brushing the
pastry

FOR THE PASTRY

225 g plain flour

2 whole eggs

2 tablespoons extra virgin olive oil

salt

iced water

Serves: 4
Preparation time: 45 minutes
Cooking time: 45 minutes

Preheat the oven to 180°C/350°F/Gas Mark 4.

In a heavy-bottomed saucepan heat the oil on a low heat and sweat the onions until very soft. Add the sieved tomatoes and simmer gently for 15 minutes, adding a little stock or water if it becomes too dry.

Remove the skins from the potatoes whilst still warm and mash with the butter, onion mixture and Pecorino and Parmigiano. Add the egg yolk and season to taste.

To make the pastry mix the flour, eggs, oil and salt and add just enough water to make a stiff dough. Using a pasta machine or heavy rolling pin if you don't have one, roll the pastry very finely and line several oiled baking trays, allowing the pastry to overlap by about 2.5 cm all the way round. Spoon the mashed potato about 2.5 cm deep over the pastry base then fold the overlapping pastry around the edges and brush with a beaten egg. Place in the centre of the oven for 30 minutes until the Torta is golden brown. To serve, allow to cool slightly and cut into 8 cm squares.

Marco *arco* " Again we find ourselves in Parma, Emiglia Romagna, whose cooks have a seemingly inbred capacity to create wonderful savoury snacks. Torta di Patate is seen in shops throughout Parma, though nowhere else in Italy. It can be made with either spinach or onion, which is the one we have here, and should be eaten warm with lots of wine and good company. This recipe was donated by Mrs Bruna Antonioni. "

BAGNA CAUDA

Anchovy, chilli and garlic dip

50 g butter
225 ml extra virgin olive oil
6 anchovy fillets
6 garlic cloves, finely chopped
juice of 1 lemon

Serves: 4
Preparation time: 5 minutes
Cooking time: 5 minutes

In a small saucepan, heat the butter and oil. Add the anchovy fillets with a little of their oil and the garlic and cook over a very low heat until the anchovies disintegrate. Simmer for another minute or two, add the lemon juice and serve with cubes of bread or chopped vegetables for dipping.

Marco " This is the perfect dip as it goes with just about everything. I have a real aversion to the manufactured dips that you find in the chill cabinet in supermarkets, which are crammed with E-numbers and additives. This is the only dip you'll ever need and is sensational as a pre-dinner nibble. "

TORTA AL LIMON

ERA CARAMEL

CIOCCOLATO REALE

DOLCI
DESSERTS

ZABAIONE

TIRAMISU

MASCARPONE CRÈME BRÛLÉE

MOUSSE DI CIOCCOLATO
Chocolate mousse

CROSTATA DI FRUTTA
Open fruit tart

CRÈME CARAMEL

SEMI-FREDDO DI BISCOTTI
Semi-freddo biscuit glacé

ZABAIONE

9 egg yolks
9 tablespoons caster sugar
225 ml Marsala wine
32 morello cherries
8 Savoyard biscuits

Serves: 4
Preparation time: 2 minutes
Cooking time: 5 minutes

Quarter fill a medium saucepan with cold water and heat to a steady simmer.

Combine the egg yolks and sugar in a glass bowl and place over the simmering water, stirring constantly, until the mixture thickens slightly.

Stirring more vigorously, trickle in the Marsala and then, using a hand-held whisk, beat the mixture until it is pale gold in colour and thick and creamy.

Serve immediately in 4 glass dishes or bowls with 8 morello cherries at the bottom of each dish and a couple of Savoyard biscuits on the side.

Marco " Zabaione originates from southern Italy and Marsala, the wine that gives it its distinctive taste, is also the name of a Sicilian city. For me, it's the perfect dessert: light and creamy, without being too rich or cloying, and with a nice alcohol kick at the end. I like mine served with Savoyard biscuits and a glass of the sweet Italian dessert wine, Vin Santo. "

TIRAMISU

40 g caster sugar
1 egg yolk
2 teaspoons Marsala wine
50 ml double cream
300 g mascarpone
8 Savoyard biscuits
cocoa powder, to serve

FOR THE BISCUIT MARINADE:
300 ml boiling water
1 dessert spoon instant coffee
50 g caster sugar
2 teaspoons Marsala wine

Serves: 4
Preparation time: 30 minutes
Chilling time: 3 hours

Start by putting all the ingredients for the biscuit marinade into a small saucepan and bring to the boil. Set aside to cool.

Next take 2 bowls and place 20 g of caster sugar in each. In the first bowl, place 1 egg yolk and the Marsala; whisk until creamy. In the second bowl, pour in the double cream and whisk until it thickens.

Take a third bowl and scoop in the mascarpone. Briskly whisk it, adding the contents of the 2 other bowls. Keep whisking until everything is combined. Dip the Savoyard biscuits into the cooled marinade for 10 seconds on each side then place on a plate.

Serve the Tiramisu either in a 20 cm shallow glass dish or in 4 individual cocktail glasses. Whichever you prefer, line the dish or glasses with enough of the biscuits to cover the bottom. Before you add each one, gently squeeze out some of the marinade. Top with a layer of mascarpone cream then repeat the process.

Finish by dusting the top with sieved cocoa powder. Chill for at least 3 hours before serving.

Frankie “ Tiramisu is the most popular pudding to come out of Italy and for good reason: when it's properly made it's as light as air and tastes divine – a true pick-me-up, as its name translates. Some people substitute sponge fingers for the Savoyard biscuits, but they just don't work as well – Savoyard biscuits are definitely worth a visit to your local deli for. The mascarpone and Marsala are non-negotiable ”

MASCARPONE CRÈME BRÛLÉE

200 g mascarpone

600 ml double cream

1 vanilla pod, split and seeds
   removed

5 egg yolks

120 g caster sugar, plus a little extra
   to serve

Serves 4

Preparation time: 10 minutes

Cooking time: 40 minutes

Setting time: 3 hours

Preheat the oven to 110°C/225°F/¼ Gas Mark.

Place the mascarpone, double cream and vanilla pod into a saucepan and bring to the boil. In a bowl, whisk together the egg yolks and caster sugar until thick and golden. Stir 1 tablespoon of the hot cream mixture into the egg yolks, then add the rest of the cream mixture, whisk thoroughly and pass through a sieve. Pour the mixture into 4 cocotte dishes and place in the oven for 35 minutes exactly. Set aside to cool then put in the fridge to set for 3 hours.

To serve, sprinkle with caster sugar and brown the topping for 2–3 minutes under a very hot grill or with a kitchen blow torch.

Marco " Whilst crème brûlée is clearly a French dish, it is also perennially popular. I have adapted it all'italiana for the Frankie's menu by adding mascarpone cheese which gives the crème brûlée a creamier, more indulgent consistency. "

201

MOUSSE DI CIOCCOLATO

Chocolate mousse

100 g good quality 55% dark
   chocolate, roughly chopped
10 g unsalted butter
3 egg whites
10 g caster sugar
1 egg yolk
25 ml espresso coffee
whipped cream, to serve.

Serves: 4
Preparation time: 15 minutes
Setting time: 2 hours

Melt the chocolate and butter in a bowl over a pan of warm water. Whisk the egg whites until they form stiff peaks, then gradually add in the caster sugar, whisking all the time. Fold the egg whites into the chocolate mixture, and then stir in the egg yolk and coffee, until smooth. Pour the mixture into 4 small bowls or ramekins and place in the fridge until set. Top with a swirl of whipped cream and serve.

Frankie " The thought of my mother's chocolate mousse can make my mouth water all the way from Italy to Newmarket. She doesn't make it often but when she does no one can resist it. "

202

CROSTATA DI FRUTTA

Open fruit tart

100 g self-raising flour
200 g plain flour
150 g unsalted butter, softened
3 egg yolks
150 g caster sugar
1 lemon, peel grated very finely
    and juiced
200 g fresh plums, stoned and
    halved, poached for about
    15 minutes in a little water
    until just tender
2 egg yolks

Serves: 4
Preparation time: 3 hours
Cooking time: 40 minutes

Preheat the oven to 180°C/350°F/Gas Mark 4.

Sift the flour then pulse the butter and flour in a food processor until it resembles fine breadcrumbs. Add the egg yolks and the sugar and blitz until smooth, then add the lemon rind and juice, blitz again and remove from the food processor. Cover and chill for at least 2 hours in the fridge.

Once the dough has rested, remove from the fridge and leave for 20 minutes until it returns to room temperature. On a floured surface, roll out the dough to the desired thickness using all the flour you need to stop it sticking. Once rolled transfer it to a 24 cm baking tin, preferably round or rectangular. Trim off the excess dough and quickly knead the trimmings together. Roll them out again and cut into identical strips. Spread the plums, cut side down, evenly over the onto the crust. Decorate the top of the pie with a lattice of dough strips. Glaze with the egg yolks and bake for around 30 minutes until golden brown.

Allow to cool before eating.

Marco " Crostata is one of the simplest Italian desserts yet is perennially popular all over Italy with each region, as ever, insisting theirs is the best. It is traditionally made with 'pasta frolla' (short-crust pastry) flavoured with lemon rind or, as you move further south, vanilla or cinnamon. My grandmother used to make one of these every Saturday with bittersweet homemade plum jam – fabulous. If you use jam make sure it's top notch, the sort you eat with a spoon late at night. Failing that, I prefer fresh fruits, the kind with a stone in, such as plums, peaches or apricots. "

CRÈME CARAMEL

225 ml milk
120 g caster sugar
1 whole egg
1 egg yolk
2 teaspoons vanilla essence

FOR THE CARAMEL:
120 g caster sugar
25 ml water

Serves: 4
Preparation time: 20 minutes
Cooking time: 1 hour 5 minutes
Setting time: 3 hours

Heat the oven to 110°C/225°F/Gas Mark ¼.

Whisk together the milk, caster sugar, whole egg, egg yolk and vanilla essence, and pass the mixture through a sieve. For the caramel topping, mix together the caster sugar and water in a heavy-bottomed saucepan over a low heat for a few minutes until the sugar dissolves and a dark caramel is formed. Pour the caramel into 4 ramekin dishes and allow to set (about 15 minutes at room temperature). Once it has solidified, pour over the egg mixture, and place the ramekins in a deep metal tray with 2.5 cm of boiling water in it. Bake in the oven for 1 hour and 5 minutes exactly. Allow to cool, then refrigerate for 3 hours. To serve, run a sharp knife around the edge of the ramekin and turn out each pudding onto a plate.

Marco " Crème caramel was Dad's staple Sunday lunch dessert. We'd always have a full Sunday roast with all the trimmings and this to follow. I love the smell of burnt sugar that fills the house whilst it's cooking. "

SEMI-FREDDO DI BISCOTTI

Semi-freddo biscuit glacé

350 ml double cream
6 egg whites
150 g caster sugar
325 g caster sugar
100 g peeled hazelnuts, roasted

FOR THE COULIS:
300 g raspberries
200 g caster sugar

Serves 10
Preparation time: 30 minutes
Freezing time: 6 hours

Put a 30 cm loaf tin into the freezer. In a bowl, whisk the double cream until it starts to thicken. In another bowl, beat the egg whites to stiff peaks, then slowly sift in the caster sugar. Fold in the double cream and set aside.

Lightly oil a heatproof surface, or greaseproof paper on a heatproof surface, with a drizzle of olive oil. Heat the sugar in a pan until caramelized then add the hazelnuts. Pour over the marble surface or greaseproof paper. Set aside to harden.

Using a rolling pin, lightly crush the hazelnuts to break up the caramel, then fold through the cream mixture. Spoon into the loaf tin and freeze for 6 hours.

To make the coulis, blend together the raspberries and the sugar in a food processor, then strain through a fine sieve and refrigerate until you are ready to serve the semi-freddo.

To serve, turn the semi-freddo out of the tin, slice into portions and drizzle the coulis over them.

Frankie " Semi-freddo literally translated means 'half cold', which is exactly what this dessert is – it's half cake, half ice cream. Catherine and I tend to serve this when we have dinner parties and you can make it well in advance and stick it in the freezer until you need it. "

207

GELATI

ICE CREAMS

GELATO DI FRAGOLA
Strawberry ice cream

GELATO ALLA VANIGLIA
CON CIOCCOLATO CALDO
Vanilla ice cream
with hot chocolate sauce

GELATO DI MELONE
Melon ice cream

SORBETTO ALLA CANNELLA
Cinnamon sorbet

GRANITA AL CAFFÉ
Coffee granita

GELATO DI FRAGOLA

Strawberry ice cream

750 g fresh ripe strawberries,
   hulled
200 g sugar
2 tablespoons caster sugar
2 tablespoons lemon juice
300 ml extra thick double cream

Serves: 6
Preparation time: 15 minutes
Freezing time: 6 hours

Roughly mash the strawberries, sprinkle with the sugar and lemon juice and leave to macerate for 1 hour. Purée the mixture and press through a sieve lined with muslin to remove the seeds and then fold in the double cream, mixing well. Place in the freezer for 6 hours, stirring thoroughly every 30 minutes.

Frankie " There is nothing in the world that tastes as good as Italian ice cream 'fatt'in casa', that is to say 'homemade'. Gelaterie in Italy are on every street corner and 'andare a prendere un gelato' (going for an ice cream) is the equivalent of going for a pint. I make my own and these recipes are simple, especially if you have an ice cream maker. "

GELATO ALLA VANIGLIA CON CIOCCOLATO CALDO

Vanilla ice cream with hot chocolate sauce

125 ml milk
375 ml double cream
1 vanilla pod, split and seeds
   removed
½ teaspoon vanilla essence
100 g caster sugar
5 eggs yolks

FOR THE CHOCOLATE SAUCE:

100 g good quality dark chocolate,
   roughly chopped
100 ml milk
100 ml double cream

Preparation time: 5 minutes
Cooking time: 15 minutes
Freezing time: 6 hours

In a heavy-bottomed saucepan, add the milk, double cream, vanilla pod and vanilla essence, bring to the boil and then remove from the heat. Whisk the sugar and eggs yolks in a bowl until thick and pale gold in colour. Add a tablespoon of the hot cream mixture, and whisk well. Then place into the saucepan and stir over a low heat until the combined mixture is thick enough to coat the back of a wooden spoon. Strain through a sieve and allow to cool. Once cooled, place in a stainless steel bowl in the freezer for 6 hours, stirring once every 30 minutes until the ice cream thickens.

Melt the chocolate in a bowl over a pan of warm water. In a saucepan, bring the milk and double cream to the boil, add the melted chocolate, then whisk and strain through a sieve.

To serve, place scoops of the ice cream in a dish with the hot chocolate sauce served separately to allow family and friends to help themselves.

$\mathcal{M}$*arco* " A real kids' favourite and the adults are keen on it too. If I'm having this with the kids at home, I've been known to pour a small jigger of brandy over my own portion before adding the chocolate sauce. "

GELATO DI MELONE

Melon ice cream

2 ripe melons
120 g caster sugar
juice of 1 whole lemon
400 ml double cream

Serves: 6
Preparation time: 15 minutes
Freezing time: 6 hours

Cut the melon into segments, discarding the skin and seeds. Cut into chunks and sprinkle with the sugar and lemon juice. Leave to stand for 1 hour, then purée thoroughly. Heat the cream gently (do not boil) then stir it into the purée. Leave the mixture to cool then place in the freezer for 6 hours, stirring thoroughly every 30 minutes.

Marco " A wonderfully fragrant and refreshing ice cream for a hot summer's day. "

SORBETTO ALLA CANNELLA

Cinnamon sorbet

3 sticks of cinnamon
500 ml water
150 g sugar
50 ml Martini Bianco
   (sweet white vermouth)

Serves: 4
Preparation time: 15 minutes
Soaking time: overnight
Freezing time: 6 hours

Soak the cinnamon sticks in the water overnight. Next day bring the water to the boil then remove from the heat. Add the sugar and the vermouth and stir to dissolve, then discard the cinnamon sticks and leave to cool. Place in freezer for 6 hours, stirring every 30 minutes.

" A really unusual flavour that packs quite a punch. Very grown up and refreshing. "

GRANITA AL CAFFÉ

Coffee granita

125 g caster sugar
125 ml very strong espresso coffee,
    freshly brewed
350 ml water
1 tablespoon Sambuca
whipped cream, to serve

Dissolve the sugar into the hot coffee, add the water and Sambuca and allow to cool. Pour into a shallow plastic container and freeze for 40 minutes. When the edges of the granita are frozen stir the mixture to break up the ice crystals, return to the freezer and repeat the process every 20 minutes for the next few hours or until the granita has set. Serve in tall glasses with long spoons, topped with whipped cream.

Serves: 4
Preparation time: 20 minutes
Setting time: 8 hours

Frankie " Italians will order this instead of their regular espresso on a hot summer's day, as you get the same caffeine kick plus a refreshing ice cream all rolled into one. "

INDEX